HEALING
WITHOUT
FEAR

HEALING
WITHOUT
FEAR

How to Overcome
Your Fear of Doctors,
Hospitals, and the
Health Care System
and Find Your Way
to True Healing

Laurel Ann Reinhardt, Ph.D.

Healing Arts Press
Rochester, Vermont

Healing Arts Press
One Park Street
Rochester, Vermont 05767
www.InnerTraditions.com

Healing Arts Press is a division of Inner Traditions International

Library of Congress Cataloging-in-Publication Data
Reinhardt, Laurel Ann, 1950-
   Healing without fear : how to overcome your fear of doctors,
hospitals, and the health care system and find your way to true healing
/ Laurel Ann Reinhardt ; foreword by James Jealous.
      p. cm.
Includes bibliographical references and index.
 ISBN 0-89281-992-8
 1. Fear of doctors. 2. Patients—Psychology. I. Title.
 R727.37 .R45 2002

                         2002010509

Printed and bound in the United States at Lake Book Manufacturing, Inc.

10 9 8 7 6 5 4 3 2 1

Text design and layout by Rachel Goldenberg
This book was typeset in Janson with Avenir as the display typeface

Contents

Acknowledgments

I want to express my gratitude to the following people, without whose help this book would never have been written or published:

All of the friends and healers who loved and truly supported me by allowing me to find my own way through two health care crises; a special thank you to Ellen.

All of the people who allowed me to interview them, whether or not their stories appear in this book; they are both courageous and inspiring.

All of my friends and colleagues who kept encouraging me to continue with this book, even through the most difficult of times; a special thank you to Claire.

All of the people at Healing Arts Press who believed in and helped bring this book to publication, looking and reading even better than I had imagined it.

Foreword

Fear is something we all experience, but individual relationships with fear vary considerably. As a general practitioner of osteopathy for more than twenty-five years, I have had intimate conversations with thousands of unique individuals about their fear and their relationship to it. Fear can vary in nature from an acute emergent terror to a chronic subliminal and almost imperceptible fear that is so much a part of the individual that it remains constant and unnoticed. Under natural conditions fear comes and goes along with life's surprises. When fear becomes steady and unyielding, successful resolution is proportionate to the health of our perceptual integrity and stability.

I practice among the rural natives of Maine, and I observe them living on the land, where they are deeply aware of the seasons, of changing weather, and of the inconvenience of natural events. When we live in rhythm with nature and her moods, a natural perceptual balance between ourselves and something greater is constantly nurtured. When our attention is focused not only on the event at hand but also on the "background," a certain balance is maintained that allows us to observe our fear in a broader context. This perceptual integrity is an essential feature of how we respond to, integrate, and understand fear and its true meaning.

Animals in the wild have this perceptual integrity. They are, like my rural neighbors, alert and uniquely balanced individuals. When sensing danger these wonderful creatures become still, heighten their senses, wait, and collect the moment in its wholeness, and then act instinctively toward a sense of continuum and wisdom. Waiting is a key element in responding to the unexpected. In the case of human illness, fear can run wild and we may make irrational decisions by being overly rational about the situation. Waiting and allowing intuition and instinct to contribute to our response often yields an unexpected ease of action. We become allies to ourselves, embraced by the calming tempo of patience.

Fear brings us knowledge. If we squirm away from it our senses will collapse and fail. If we wait we find that fear brings us to a deeper trust, delivering us from the grip of rational ambivalence with its frightening need to be immediately comfortable and subdued by denial.

My personal experience with both friends and patients has taught me that the root of fear is a separation from the Wholeness of Love. Fear arises when we lose our sense of the Divine Background, when we shrink our perceptual field to the point where we are alone, coldly isolated from the wider peripheral sense of nature's rhythms and the divine warmth of Oneness. Fear in all its varieties reminds us that something is missing, and eventually we come to a point of memory that speaks to us so deeply that a softness pervades the sharpness of fear and we sense the healing light of a widening vista and the divine embrace of freedom.

Fear is the friend ringing the doorbell of our being, hoping for someone to answer. Our task is to hear this call and wait with a wider vision until a natural balance emerges from the instinctual core of our being. This is not faith—it is an instinctual knowing of one's origin in the womb of life, and it produces an awareness that carries us into calm.

JAMES JEALOUS, D.O.
EASTON, N.H.

Introduction

A few years ago I had the opportunity to experience all the aspects of fear that Dr. Jealous describes in the Foreword—as well as an additional aspect. One morning in December 1996, I found, as have millions of women and men before and since, a lump in my breast. Even as I poked and prodded, hoping that my untrained fingers would discover they had been mistaken, my mind had already leapt to the assumption that the lump was cancer and that something needed to be done—immediately. I quickly entered what I now think of as the "field of fear," which I believe pervades health care in the United States and which dogged me at every turn for the next several days, weeks, and months. Though at first I believed it to be entirely my own fear, I gradually realized that it was, in fact, a field of fear, an "entity" that fed not just on my fears but on those of others as well.

*Be prepared
To risk everything you
Hold precious
For the truth inside you.
TRUTH is Empowering
And to speak the truth
Is to overcome the fear
of death.*

—Jane Evershed,
"Truth Visiting"

MY PERSONAL STORY

I have spent the last two decades using what are generally considered to be alternative or complementary types of health care, including osteopathy, chiropractic, homeopathy, and Asian medicine (for example, acupuncture, herbs, and Qigong). I now realize that I discontinued my use of Western medicine precisely because of the field of fear that surrounds it, though I didn't define it that way at the time. This is not to say that alternative health care doesn't contribute its own set of fears to the field of fear, but in my experience the field is much less palpable in alternative health care.

In the early 1980s I struggled with pneumonia every fall for three years. After the last bout I ended up developing what my doctor referred to as a type of asthma that was primarily exercise-induced. I was given an inhalant (which I later found was rumored to be carcinogenic) and was urged to use it prophylactically—that is, before exercising. I was also told that there was nothing else to be done. Unwilling to live the rest of my life that way—I was barely in my thirties and wanted to continue enjoying such activities as tennis and skiing—I elected to get a second opinion from a homeopath. The remedy he gave me immediately eased my symptoms, and I never looked back.

I didn't look back, that is, until I found the lump in my breast and once again felt the fear rising up within me. Perhaps it was this fear and its association with Western medicine that sent me running back to a Western medical doctor. Although I didn't have a personal physician, I thought I knew of one who would be able to see me for who I was and work with me in ways that would feel comfortable for and respectful to both of us. What I hadn't considered was the field of fear, within which the doctor practiced her art and which limited her as much as it threatened me.

Within a few minutes of entering the doctor's office I felt as if I had been dropped onto a bobsled that was heading straight down a mountain. The first indication was in the waiting room, where I began to feel a vague disquiet. As I was shown to a treatment room, I mentioned to the nurse that I was hoping to have a Pap smear as well as a breast exam. She checked my chart and informed me in a brusque, hurried, fearful manner, that I had been scheduled for two time units rather than the three that were required for a Pap smear. I felt my disquiet turn into apprehension; what if I couldn't get all my questions answered in the two allotted time units?

When the doctor arrived, she did not immediately assuage my anxieties, as I had hoped she would. She felt my breast, indicated that it was not the type of lump she could quickly discount, and recommended I get a mammogram and follow up with a surgical consultation. I didn't ask her about alternatives to having such a sensitive area of the body irradiated, or if the results of that procedure would really make a difference to her or the surgeon, or if I could put off seeing a surgeon while I tried some alternatives; I simply acceded to her recommendations out of fear.

In my rush to keep the tests moving along as quickly as possible, I ended up having the mammogram on the Winter Solstice, the longest night of the year and a very important spiritual holiday for me—and an apt metaphor. Fortunately, a friend offered to drive me to the clinic, which was actually a mobile van. The technicians were wonderful, but the equipment, the confined space, and the procedure itself added to my anxiety and fear. Furthermore, I wasn't able to get the results immediately; in fact, something went awry with the clinic's notification system and I never received the postcard saying that the mammogram was negative, which would have helped to calm me.

The longer I waited, the more fearful I became, and I didn't have the presence of mind or background to use that time to delve deep inside and check in with my internal senses. Instead I spent ten excruciating days waiting to hear from the surgeon, and when I visited her office her bedside manner did nothing to calm me. Without asking permission or explaining her intention, she prepared to aspirate, or draw fluid from, the lump. If she was able to draw fluid from and collapse the lump, a friend had explained the night before, it would be a good sign; the doctor made no reference to this. I consented to the procedure out of fear. I was hoping the lump could be aspirated, as

The High Stakes of Western Medicine:
A Dream

In addition to my personal experience with the field of fear in medicine, I had a dream during my healing process that alerted me to many facets of this field:

I am at a high-class, high-stakes party. Someone who looks exactly like Jamie Lee Curtis is there. She is wearing an old-style nurse's uniform, like Florence Nightingale's, complete with cap and cape, but it is all black. It is also very gauzy—you can see right through to her black, lacy underwear. She is very seductive.

She decides to leave. She heads down the stairway to the front door. As she goes down the stairs she casts a gigantic shadow on the wall. Suddenly I am down on the street beside her, but invisible to her. She seems to have some sense of foreboding as she whispers her destination to the taxi driver then looks over her shoulder to see if she is being followed. The taxi driver says he can make sure they are not followed, and he begins a series of intricate turns designed to lose pursuers. I have the sense, however, that this will not help, and it will be only a matter of time before the nurse is found and eliminated.

The setting of the dream is a party, a very special kind of party that is full of high rollers. Because of "Florence Nightingale's" attendance, I assume the high rollers are VIPs of the health care industry; I also assume they are (covertly) discussing business.

Florence Nightingale (1820-1910) was a famous British army nurse who has become an archetype of Western medicine; she represents health care at its best, in its most idealized aspect. She was the selfless nurse who took care of men on the field of battle, itself a field of fear. Interestingly, war has become a metaphor for what goes on in Western medicine—the "war on cancer," "attack the cells," "search and destroy," and so forth.

This dream figure is a very different Florence Nightingale. She wears similar clothes, but her outfit is seductive. Western medicine is very seductive; it has achieved some major successes. And I had recently been seduced back into its fold, however briefly. But the nurse's outfit is also transparent. Problems in the system have become so bad that it is obvious to everyone that something is wrong. In the dream I "hitch a ride" with Western medicine, but I am unseen by her, just as my intuitions, feelings, and needs are largely ignored by Western physicians.

Jamie Lee Curtis is an interesting choice to play the part of Florence Nightingale. When I free-associated to the actor, I thought of her first major role in the movie *Halloween*, as the strong teenager who is terrorized by a killer but eventually prevails (much like the real Nightingale whose work was scoffed at by battlefield physicians and officers), and her role as the "abandoned" wife of Arnold Schwarzenegger in *True Lies*.

I wonder about the phrase *true lies*. It seems like an oxymoron, a paradox, but it feels like part of what is going on in health care right now. There are "truths" that are true for some people while they are lies for other people, and yet there is an attempt to apply these "truths" to everyone. This is, perhaps, the biggest lie in health care: that one size fits all, or that there is only one true way to practice medicine, provide health care, or achieve health.

When she leaves the party, Florence Nightingale casts a huge shadow on the wall. In Jungian psychology the shadow is an archetype, the unconscious aspect of ourselves that carries the "good" and "bad" pieces of ourselves to which we are reluctant or unable to admit. Interestingly, Florence Nightingale and her services were initially rejected by the military officers and medical consultants, who felt that her ideas about cleanliness, nutrition, and caring for the sick on the field of battle were both theoretically foolish and dangerous to morale; they didn't want the men to be coddled or spoiled. Nightingale finally prevailed because she trusted and stuck to her instincts, which turned out to be right. I believe this is a huge part of the shadow—the fear—of Western medicine: that we rely on and feel safer with our technology and statistics as opposed to our instincts, intuition, and good old-fashioned caring. Or, as Dr. Jealous calls it, the Wholeness of Love.

this would allay my fear. But when the doctor couldn't draw fluid, my fear increased substantially.

The surgeon recommended a lumpectomy and began checking her schedule for the time to do it. If I had been alone and if it had not been New Year's Eve day, I would have tried to schedule this procedure for the very next day, again because of fear. But my friend reminded me that I had some questions to ask. One of these queries was about options, including alternatives to surgery. Though the surgeon grudgingly agreed that I could "safely" take up to three months to try some other options, her demeanor clearly indicated she thought this was a bad idea, and she had no recommendations regarding what those alternatives might be.

That was one of the scariest days of my life. I wanted desperately to live, but I was afraid of what living might entail from that moment forward—the pain I might have to endure, the endless medical procedures, the indignities, the anxiety that made me want to crawl out of my skin, the loneliness and "aloneness," the deep sadness and grief that I might not see what I then considered my life's work come to fruition. I was also afraid of the possibility that who I was—generally a self-assured, intuitive, and inner-directed person—would completely disappear in the face of the irresistible forces of fear and the Western medical system. I didn't know what to do. I went home to consider my options. I began by opening my journal and rediscovering what I had written just that morning.

I had awakened with an image of a joyous outdoor celebration, which I had interpreted both personally, as a good outcome with the surgeon, and communally, as the St. Paul Capitol New Year's Eve Party, which I planned to attend with friends that night. After the surgical consultation I didn't feel like going; I couldn't find anything worth celebrating, and I thought I might feel even more alone in a crowd of strangers. But I kept coming back to the image of that morning, struggling to find its meaning and value for me.

Finally, after two weeks of having trusted doctors and feeling progressively worse and more fearful, I decided to trust the image my own psyche had produced. I went to the party, where I was given the responsibility of helping with a candlelight procession through downtown St. Paul to a park with a gigantic bonfire. There, people were encouraged to burn away their fears. So instead of being at home in a field of fear, I found myself in a field of pure joy, love, and celebration. This was the doorway that allowed me to exit from that field of fear. This journey toward love and discovering more of my essence is still going on today.

The next day I called a Vietnamese acupuncturist with whom I had previously worked. His first words were, "Don't be afraid; fear makes disease stronger." I appreciated this articulation of my own developing awareness. I got some herbs from him, and some dietary recommendations from a naturopath. I slowed down and took some extra time for listening to and nurturing myself. I asked my friends to send me their love—an unusual request for me, but it felt like the right thing to do. I had begun trusting myself, my dreams, my own ways of "knowing" again.

One dream in particular fortified my growing sense of calm. I was walking around town and shopping with a knife in my hand. Suddenly I realized that I didn't need to carry a knife around just to shop, so I asked a shopkeeper to hold it for me. When I went back to retrieve the knife it was broken in two and totally unusable. In the dream I decided I didn't need the knife at all and I threw it away. Upon waking I took this to mean I didn't need a surgeon's knife in the current course of my life. (For another dream I had that prompted me to begin writing about my experiences, please see the sidebar The High Stakes of Western Medicine: A Dream on page 4.) I also wrote a poem (see Schroedinger's Lump, page 92), which became a mantra for me about my decision not to have surgery. Later, just within the amount of time the surgeon had given me to explore other options, the lump was gone. It remains absent to this day.

HEALING

In many respects, how we heal is a mystery. According to many traditions—most notably Eastern, but also several Western traditions such as chiropractic, osteopathy, homeopathy, and midwifery—the human mind, body, and spirit are connected as one and are capable of healing themselves.

To illustrate, think of the last time you cut yourself. Although you might have consciously helped the process of healing by washing and bandaging the wound, your body, mind, spirit already knew how to heal that cut, just as you know how to birth a baby or mend a broken bone. We have all heard stories of seemingly miraculous healings; we have also heard of or even experienced firsthand situations in which healing appears not to have happened or seems to have gone awry, resulting in chronic illness or premature death.

In this book the term *healing* is not being used synonymously with *curing*, which is about relieving the signs and symptoms of disease. Instead I use *healing* to refer to the process of deepening our understanding of ourselves, expressing more of our true nature (including our own ways of knowing), and moving closer to wholeness. Healing has different meanings for different people; for some it means returning to their predisease level of health or better, and for others it means living a quality life with a chronic illness or experiencing a meaningful death.

Why We Don't Heal

There are many theories about why healing does or doesn't take place. Caroline Myss contends that many of us don't heal because we actively yet unconsciously use our psychic wounds to engage others in enabling us to maintain the status quo—a form of collusion.[1] I think the collusion is much broader and deeper than Myss suggests, extending to include not only our friends, families, health care practitioners, insurance brokers, advertisers, and journalists who write about health care, but also all people who have ever had diseases even remotely similar to ours. This is a collusion of silence, fear, and disempowerment of ourselves and each other that creates a morphic field of fear surrounding the Western health care system in general and some illnesses, such as cancer and AIDS, in particular.

I am not referring to the personal fears and anxieties that often alert us to problems within our bodies, minds, and spirits, urge us to seek help once we know that a problem exists, or open us to the deeper awareness that facilitates true healing. Instead, I am alluding to an energetic, emotional field of fear that surrounds and permeates the practice of Western medicine and actively hinders the healing process. This was the fear I experienced the day I found the lump in my breast, and it left me paralyzed and unable to pause and reflect.

MORPHIC FIELDS:
THE STORY OF THE HUNDREDTH MONKEY[2]

This story is said to be true.

Once upon a time some scientists were studying several bands of monkeys on a group of islands. The scientists were dropping food rations, in the form of a burlap sack of potatoes, on each island daily.

One day, one of the bags broke open close to the shoreline and a potato rolled into the ocean. The monkey that ate this potato apparently liked the salty taste, and the next day he was observed dipping his potato in the ocean before eating it. Being great copycats several of the other monkeys began dipping their potatoes in the ocean the following day. Each day more and more monkeys on that island followed suit, until all 100 monkeys were doing it. When the hundredth monkey dipped his potato in the ocean, monkeys on several neighboring islands, who could not possibly have seen this behavior, spontaneously began dipping their potatoes in the ocean before eating them. Thus morphic fields are generated.

According to Rupert Sheldrake, an eminent British botanist and expert on morphic fields:

> The nature of things depends on fields, called morphic fields. Each kind of natural system has its own kind of field: there is an insulin field, a beech [tree] field, a swallow field, and so on. Such fields shape all the different kinds of atoms, molecules, crystals, living organisms, societies, customs, and habits of mind. . . . [These] fields, like the known fields of physics, are non-material regions of influence extending in space and continuing in time. They are localized within and around the systems they organize.[3]

What Sheldrake means is that who we are genetically, behaviorally, and emotionally is influenced by those morphic fields with which we have resonance. Generally, each of us is most resonant with our own past experiences and behaviors, like the fear I had previously felt in connection with my experiences with Western medicine. However, says Sheldrake:

> Morphic resonance takes place on the basis of similarity. The more similar an organism is to previous organisms, the greater their influence on it by morphic resonance. And the more such organisms there have been, the more powerful their cumulative influence.[4]

So who I am is impacted not only by my own past experience and behavior, but also by that of my parents and grandparents, my larger ethnic group, my various cultural groups (that is, the types of people with whom I associate at school, business, church, and so on), and any other groups with whom I share some commonalities—such as people who like cats. The magnitude of the influence is determined by the degree of our similarities and the sizes of the groups involved. Thus my fear would have resonated with and been augmented by: all my past experiences with fear, my mother's fear of life and my father's fear of death, the fears of the millions of people who had at some point found lumps in their breasts, the fears of people who had actually had cancer, the fears of all my family members and friends, the fears of oncologists and other health care workers, and so forth.

> *The field of fear in medicine is real.*
>
> —LARRY DOSSEY, M.D.,
> FROM A LETTER

A Morphic Field of Fear

I believe a morphic field of fear surrounds the practice of medicine, Western medicine in particular, and that this field negatively affects our abilities to heal. This field is created by the following non-exhaustive list of factors:

- the personal fears we each have about pain, illness, disability, life, and death
- the fears of doctors that we assimilate, sometimes called "white coat fever"
- doctors' fears of making mistakes, failing their patients, or being sued
- fear-based methods of teaching and practicing medicine
- financial fears of patients, doctors, insurance companies, and the government
- fear-based sales tactics of insurance companies and advertisers
- cultural, including religious or spiritual, fears
- fears engendered by media reports on health care topics
- fears of loss of power and control

- fears of the unknown
- all of the above fears going back to the very beginnings of medicine

Though the morphic field of fear is usually triggered by our own fears, it can then multiply our fears exponentially, to the point where all that is experienced is fear. This makes it much more difficult for patients and doctors alike to heal, because the level of fear makes it impossible for us to listen to ourselves; our bodies, minds, and spirits; our healing intuitions and instincts; and each other. Even if we begin without fear, the field of fear in a doctor's office or hospital is often palpable and can induce that fear within us. Consider the last time you visited someone in the hospital; did you start to feel anxious, panicky, ill, or fearful, even though you thought or knew yourself to be perfectly healthy?

WHAT FEAR HAS TO DO WITH HEALING

Illness is a sign that something is wrong. Fear is a natural first reaction to illness and can often feel like a "friend ringing the doorbell" that James Jealous speaks of, a friend who lets us know that something is missing and we need to address it. In this sense fear can be an ally. But when fear becomes steady and unyielding, becoming so familiar that we don't even notice it, it actually inhibits the healing process. This kind of fear causes us to pull back, constrict, and protect ourselves and our way of life at times when we need to move forward, expand, and open up to new possibilities.

Network Chiropractic addresses this issue directly in its very premise, which focuses on removing interference such as fear from the nervous system.

> When individuals function with a clear and flexible nervous system, they are better able to recover from life's challenges. They adapt to changes more easily and are better able to grow, heal, and evolve.[5]

The morphic field of fear surrounding health care inhibits not only our own ability to heal, but also the abilities of others to help and support us. Our friends pull back, afraid of coming too close to their own mortality, afraid of the pain of possibly losing a friend. Our families constrict, circling the wagons, so to speak, and in so doing often keep out others who might be of help to us and themselves. Our health care specialists protect themselves, their positions, and their own feelings, perhaps not wanting to care too much about the next patient who might die, perhaps worrying about making a mistake, getting sued, or losing their livelihood. The process of healing often gets lost in the shuffle.

TRANSFORMING THE FIELD OF FEAR

I have heard that only one kind of consciousness can occupy a particular space at any one time. In *Conversations with God* Neale Donald Walsch writes that there are two primary emotions or types of consciousness that rule our experiences: love and fear. (This may seem a rather simplistic view of a very complex topic, but many philosophers and theologians over the years have held similar views.) Where fear is constrictive, love is expansive; where fear undoes, love creates; where fear inhibits, love opens up. By loving your body, the people around you, your environment, your job, your life, and yourself—your whole self, including your dreams and intuitions and even your illnesses and fears—you can create a field of joy and health that fear can no longer undo. But once we are in a field of fear, what recourse do we have?

Transforming the field of fear in Western health care is an enormous undertaking, but it's a process to which each of us can contribute, thereby creating a new morphic field. This process begins by recognizing the existence of the field of fear—acknowledging its presence and its influence on our own health and the health care system itself. Each of us must take personal responsibility for our own fears and respond to those fears constructively; this means refusing to take on someone else's fear or project our fears onto others. It also means taking responsibility for our healing by acting as our own health care team leader, engaging actively in conversation

Give Up My Health Insurance?
Are You Crazy?

In the July/August 2000 issue of *Blue Ridge Country*, there was an article about Elizabeth Hunter, a woman who got rid of her health insurance. "Unwittingly I'd been feeding for decades on a steady diet of stories about fearsome diseases that urged me to monitor myself for 'danger signs,'" she told the magazine. She realized that one of the consequences of that fear was the purchase of health insurance. "Maybe that makes sense when you're young. . . . But I'm 55." She admitted that during the first few months without health insurance she felt a little edgy, but then she got used to the idea. And it freed up funds for other issues she felt were more important—like buying into a land trust in her neighborhood. It's her way of being part of the solution to the problem of pollution. "It's never going to feel good," she remarks, "But helping protect that land instead of buying health insurance: That feels some better. Salve to the wound."

with our friends, family members, and health care practitioners and expecting them to respond to us as the whole individuals we are. We must also pay as much attention to our dreams, intuition, and knowing as we do to logic, statistics, lab tests, and usual and customary treatment plans. We may even have to give up health care insurance (see sidebar above) if carrying it becomes more of a hindrance than an aid—a source of fear, rather than a source of support and relief. Ultimately, it may mean dismantling our entire health care system and starting over with one that is based on love and caring rather than on fear and curing.

Inner Traditions • Bear & Company

P.O. Box 388
Rochester, VT 05767-0388
U.S.A.

Please send us this card to receive our latest catalog.

☐ Check here if you would like to receive our catalog via e-mail.

E-mail address _____

Name _____ Company _____

Address _____ Phone _____

City _____ State ____ Zip ____ Country ____

Please check the following area(s) of interest to you:

☐ Health ☐ Self-help ☐ Spirituality ☐ Shamanism
☐ Ancient Mysteries ☐ New Age ☐ Tarot ☐ Martial Arts
☐ Spanish Language ☐ Sexuality/Drugs ☐ Children ☐ Teen

Order at 1-800-246-8648 • Fax (802) 767-3726
E-mail: orders@InnerTraditions.com • Web site: www.InnerTraditions.com

MY PROFESSIONAL STORY

Taking personal responsibility for fears is not limited to patients; it applies to family, friends, and health care professionals as well. As a health care professional, I have been aware of the field of fear in my particular arena of the health care system—psychology and psychotherapy—for more than fifteen years. I got my first inkling of its existence when I was threatened by a client; despite my colleagues' reassurances that I had done nothing wrong, I endured several weeks of nearly sleepless nights for no reason other than the increasingly litigious nature of our society and my profession.

This experience alerted me to the need to "do unto others." I realized that one of the ways I can help transform the field of fear for other professionals—and for all of us—is to make the commitment never to sue a health care practitioner frivolously or for an honest mistake. In this way I can withdraw at least one small potential source of fear. What if each of us refused to let an opportunistic lawyer turn an honest mistake or an inevitable death into a case of malpractice, just because we are too grief-stricken to know that it is really us and our fears they are preying on?

My next experience with fear came with the advent of HMOs. A few years into the new paradigm I began to hear horror stories about a particular insurance company, which was forcing some of my colleagues into bankruptcy. After agreeing to the appropriateness of therapy and reimbursing the therapists for their fees, this company changed its mind and demanded its money back. The demands were made without any concern for the therapist or the impact they might have on the client. Frightened this might happen to me and aware of some ethical conflicts, I gave up my contract with this insurance company.

But these incidents do not compare to the most insidious fear-producing situation of all: the workings of the board that had granted me my license to practice psychology. Purposely or not, this board created an atmosphere of paranoia, fear, and distrust in its licensees by such activities as conducting its investigations in private, meting out censures which often seemed out of proportion to the "offense," and not informing licensees when cases had been dismissed.

Although I had been struggling with this situation for about ten years, it recently became clear to me that I had to "walk my talk." I could no longer support the board's fear-based tactics, which create a field within which it is difficult, if not impossible, to practice a healing art such as psychotherapy. (In its literal translation from the Greek, *psychotherapy* means "to heal the soul.") Therefore, in the fall of 2001, I resigned my license. I wrote a four-page heartfelt letter to the board, stating my personal and ethical concerns. It was acknowledged only by a form letter, the contents of which merely served to confirm the correctness of my decision.

ACUTE VERSUS CHRONIC FEAR

Acute fear has a very important and useful function: it warns us of and prepares us to face situations that pose a danger to us; this is often called the fight-or-flight response. Physiologically, the energy produced by fear is meant to move through our bodies like a wave, preparing us for and then being discharged by whatever action we take. It constricts us briefly, much like the constriction a cat experiences as it prepares to pounce on prey. But just as a cat does not hold this tension for long, neither are we meant to remain in such a constricted state for more than the few moments it takes to assess a particular situation, make the choice to fight or flee, and then act on that decision. The entire universe functions on this cycle of expansion, constriction, expansion, constriction. Our breathing is an example of this.

Chronic fear, on the other hand, is fear that has not been fully discharged; instead, it has become lodged in the body and mind, keeping the body in a constant state of tension and preparedness. In this state we are less open to new information and new possibilities; our attention, whether or not we are aware of it, is always on the alert for danger. This inhibits our creativity, hampers complete relaxation, and is associated with the dis-ease of a suppressed immune system. In this book, it is chronic fear that I am concerned with.

Seven Premises about Chronic Fear

1. Fear causes us to live within a restricted circle of our potential being. Fear is constricting. It limits our creativity and ability to think "outside the box." It causes congestion and blockages in all realms of our being. Fear even suppresses the immune system and inhibits the expression of emotions such as love and compassion.

2. The limitations we experience with fear are self-perpetuating. Fear becomes a self-fulfilling prophecy; it is something familiar that we tend to embrace or even wallow in because living with it is less threatening than facing the unknown. It also keeps reappearing on anniversary dates and when we enter situations that recall the original fear.

3. Fear is largely created by the restriction or removal of options for ways of knowing or being in the world (a disconnection from self/Self/God). Carl Gustav Jung, Ken Wilber, and Carol Gilligan, among others, write eloquently about the many different ways of knowing that are available to us. For example, Jung believes that people have four main methods of experiencing the world: sensing, intuiting, feeling, and thinking. Wilber also mentions four ways (see chart below), while Gilligan identifies two: masculine and feminine. Ideally the modes are equally balanced, but most of us prefer one mode to the others. To the degree that we use only one mode, we

KEN WILBER'S WAYS OF KNOWING

		INTERNAL	EXTERNAL
I		Subjective	Objective
		Meditation	Measurement (scientific method)
		Dreams	Senses
WE		Mythology	System theory

Wilber's four quadrants of knowing/being are created by the two axes of internal/external and individual/group. Thus, there is some knowledge we can attain only by going inside ourselves, while we can attain other knowledge only in groups. Internal ways of knowing are not measurable in the Western scientific sense of that word, but they are reproducible if you follow the same methods (for instance, meditation) used by others to arrive at that particular knowing. Of course, knowing often takes many years of practice (not study). [6]

become out of balance and internal conflict arises. I believe this internal conflict is in large measure fear-based. That is, fear sets in when any of these potential ways of knowing become unavailable.

This shutting down often happens in childhood when fear-based adults, confronted by free and open children, begin to set limits. Of course, certain limits are necessary, but often these limits are arbitrary and have to do with the children's ways of knowing, which adults find threatening because they don't fit in with their world-view. When children resist giving up these parts of themselves, they are often threatened with such actions as loss of affection, physical punishment, and belittling. The child's world-view becomes in*valid*, and they start down the road toward becoming fear-based *in*valids.

The only thing to fear is fear itself.

—FRANKLIN DELANO ROOSEVELT
IN HIS FIRST
INAUGURAL ADDRESS

To define knowledge as merely empirical is to limit one's ability to know; it enfeebles one's ability to feel and think.

—WENDELL BERRY,
LIFE IS A MIRACLE:
AN ESSAY AGAINST
MODERN SUPERSTITION

I came across an interesting acronym for this situation: FEAR, which stands for False Evidence Appearing Real. As children we have a certain experience of the world. When the adults around us are uncomfortable with our perspective, think they know the "truth" and wish to enlighten us, or want to save us from the danger of finding out for ourselves, we are told that our experience is wrong or, at the very least, that it is not a useful approach to the world. Their experience, on the other hand, is right. We come to believe their ideas because we are threatened with the loss of the adult's love or approval or because the adult looks like an authority—someone who should know. We trust their evidence instead ours, but theirs is "false evidence" because it is not ours; it is not the evidence we find from our own ways of knowing.

An example of FEAR is the little girl who sucks in her stomach when her gymnastics coach tells her little girls do not have bellies, even though she knows that holding in her stomach makes her feel off balance. Another example is the little boy who turns in a beautiful painting to his teacher, only to be told that "grass is green, not blue," instead of the teacher asking why the boy is feeling a little blue that morning. Similarly, the little boy who is told by his father not to cry because "that little fall didn't hurt" experiences a diminishing of the trust of himself and his abilities. The little girl who is told by her doctor that there is nothing wrong with her when she knows she feels pain in her elbow is also being given false evidence. These types of experiences separate us not only from ourselves, but also from the Self, our experience of God.

4. Our current ground of being is fear-based.

Fear is everywhere. It has become the base mode of our existence, so much that we aren't even aware of it. It becomes readily apparent, however, if you consider the many faces of fear, which include fear, anxiety, anger, indifference, frustration, sadness, grief, obsessive/compulsive behaviors, avoidance, lack of risk taking, boredom, lying, unconsciousness, and living in the past or future. This ground of fear is also obvious if you observe the messages and images of fear with which you are bombarded on a daily basis, whether at work, at home, in church, in advertisements, in news reports, or in entertainment.[7] (See the sidebar Fear and the Media on pages 20–22 for some examples.) As an illustration of the pervasiveness of fear, on a recent trip to San Francisco, I saw a teenager with a backpack on which there was factory embroidery that read, "Fear everything."

> *I realize the disservice I did to my kids by thinking I always knew better than they did. An infant has more wisdom than we can acknowledge, and by age five most of it is subdued.*
>
> —DONNA, NURSE

> *Our institutions are all fear-based.*
>
> —LARRY WILSON, FOUNDER OF WILSON LEARNING

> *A pebble cast into a pond causes ripples that spread in all directions. Each one of our thoughts, words, and deeds is like that.*
>
> —DOROTHY DAY

5. We all contribute to this morphic field of fear.

Recent theory and research in botany, physics, physiology, and psychology, as well as ancient spiritual beliefs and mythology, suggest that we are all responsible for the creation and maintenance of the field of fear within which we currently live. We project it onto others when we blame; we

Fear and the Media

You've all seen them—the ads, magazine covers, movies that use fear to get their messages across—messages that are usually about selling something. This is especially heinous in the arena of health care. One ad demonstrates how a stroll through the park, once "dangerous" due to countless allergens such as ragweed, flower pollens, and dog dander, is made safe by drugs—assuming you are willing to ignore the three pages of disclaimers about side effects. Another ad with a gun pointed directly at you, the reader, reassures that should you be shot and paralyzed, this insurance company will help you and your family on the road to recovery. Even some public television documentaries focus on fear to drive their point home. Here we have three examples of how fear, in relation to health care, has been addressed by the media:

This cover of *Life* from a few years ago might just as well have been an ad for a drug company. It uses our fear of aging (and, by extension, rejection or abandonment for no longer looking youthful) to sell the magazine and, secondarily, to promote such things as hormone replacement therapy. Results from the latest studies on this "therapy" demonstrate how devastating the consequences of fear-based choices can be.

This headline from a newsletter for psychologists published by a professional liability insurer is a double-edged sword. While it accurately captures the level of fear that the

Protecting You
From the Managed Care Litigation Tinderbox

Managed care litigation is on the rise, so Psychologist/Attorney Bryant L. Welch offers timely suggestions to protect psychologists from liability

possibility of malpractice litigation is creating for many health care professionals and does offer some useful advice for avoiding such circumstances, it also subtly preys on those fears to sell higher levels of insurance.

This ad from NABCO recognizes and addresses breast cancer, what Caroline Myss and Norm Shealy dubbed "the epidemic of fear." With its play on words—fear less by being fearless—this ad has become a mainstay in NABCO's campaign to educate the public about the realities of breast cancer in a low-key, nonthreatening manner.

radiate it out into the environment when we live with fear rather than love in our hearts. The good news is that since we are responsible for it we can stop it. The aim of this book is both to help you become aware of the extent to which you are affected by and contribute to this field of fear and to offer methods for transforming rather than perpetuating the fear. For example, today I saw a bumper sticker that read "Encourage your hopes, not your fears."

6. **An ally can help bring us back to who we really are.** One of the reasons why we may be afraid to face our fears is that they often stir up a lot of other feelings. Having an ally helping us or simply witnessing our process can be tremendously supportive, making us feel safe and secure as we explore some very difficult feelings. This ally can be a friend, acquaintance, peer counselor, paid therapist, an experience of loving or being loved, or God. It all depends on our particular situation, needs, and proclivities.

There is another reason for working with an ally. In 1954 S.E. Asch demonstrated that individuals can be swayed to discount their own experiences when faced with an alternate majority opinion. He placed an individual in a classroom where the teacher and other students were all in on the experiment. The teacher drew two lines on the board, then asked the students which was longer. After hearing his classmates pronounce the shorter line to be longer, the unsuspecting student often gave the same answer. When a single ally (who reports his or her choice ahead of the unsuspecting student) is introduced into this situation, the rate of "error," or "abandonment of self," drops to zero. [8]

We are swayed by others' perceptions, opinions, and judgments because we don't want to be the only person holding a particular position or belief. This is probably because we are afraid of being rejected or ridiculed; a large majority of us will allow this to influence our way of being in the world—the risks we take, the stands we make. Having one ally, however, one person who agrees with us or makes it clear that his or her opinion of or love for us will not be affected by the choices we make, allows us to better stand up for ourselves in the world.

7. **Grounded, purposeful, loving movement is the key to transforming fear.** Movement, whether it be physical, emotional, energetic, mental, or spiritual, takes us out of our fear, often immediately. Fear is preparation for movement. Fear's purpose is to alert us to danger and prepare us to deal with it. It gives us the adrenaline rush we need to be able to fight an enemy or flee from danger, and then it dissipates, moving through us like a wave. Notice that both fight and flight involve movement—purposeful movement. But most of the things that trigger a fear response are not so simple to deal with; movement often does not happen, and the energy gets trapped in the body and mind rather than being released. An example of this stagnation is the fear of being raped or violated. While this fear can result in our taking the action of walking only in well-lit areas, such action often does nothing to allay the fear itself. Other examples include the fear of being downsized, the fear of making a fool of ourself or saying the wrong thing in a speech, or the fear of failure.

Movement is what can help get that energy going, ultimately releasing it from our bodies and minds. But remember the words *grounded* and *purposeful;* frantic or frenetic movement itself is fear-based. As Dr. Jealous points out in the preface, it is important to be still long enough to understand what the best response for the moment might be. The movement need not be physical: it can be mental, as in an adjustment of beliefs or attitudes; emotional, as when you cry; or spiritual, as in prayer.)

Very often movement gets thwarted by someone who holds some power or authority in our lives, or by us when we choose not to follow our own intuition. This is when chronic fear begins. When movement that is consistent with who we truly are becomes thwarted, fear gets stuck in our bodies and minds. This can manifest as physical congestion, as in a limited range of motion or chronic respiratory problems. It can manifest as mental congestion, as when we obsess over the same one or two thoughts. It can also manifest as emotional congestion, so that we seem to have a limited number of colors to our emotional palette. Or it can manifest as energetic congestion, as when we keep having the same kind of experience over and over. Finally, it can manifest as spiritual congestion, when we forget or choose not to follow through with daily or weekly spiritual practices.

How to Use This Book

Although this book is organized in chapters, the exercises may be used in any order that feels useful or appropriate. In fact, after the first step of recognizing that you are holding some fear, you may find yourself immediately propelled into one or more of the other phases. I have included a wide variety of exercises, knowing that no one exercise will work for all people, while some exercises will be helpful for just a handful of people. I encourage you to allow yourself to be drawn to particular exercises. Try those first, and then expand into other exercises as needed. You may find it helpful to take a few minutes to record some of these exercises, especially those for meditation and guided visualization. A number of the exercises involve journaling; I recommend that you buy or make a special notebook dedicated to your experiences with fear and its transformation. You can then use the journal as an ally.

God and my journal became indistinguishable.

—Gayle Foster Lewis,
from a speech at
St. Catherine University,
St. Paul, Minnesota

Although this book was written specifically for people with health and health care concerns who are experiencing debilitating fear in their healing journeys, the exercises may be used by anyone for whom fear is an issue.

The Five Rs of Fear

I have divided this workbook into four main sections—*recognizing, reporting, releasing, replacing*—that may be thought of as phases in which fear is addressed. They often overlap, however, and you may find yourself moving back and forth between the phases as you work through various issues of fear in your life. The fifth R is *responding*, which is not the same as *reacting*; when you are in this phase you are really out of the grips of chronic fear and are expressing your true self.

Do not be discouraged if you seem to find yourself repeatedly cycling back through one particular fear; we tend to have one main area of fear—our personal Achilles' heel—that continues to be triggered. Unfortunately, we seldom recognize the progress we have made and the fact that what often feels like a circle is really a spiral. That is, we may come to a place that feels familiar, so we assume we are cycling back through a place we have been before instead of realizing that we have reached a completely different level or layer. Therefore, I would recommend acknowledging yourself in some way after each step you take. Best wishes on your healing, transformative journey.

How Do I Keep the Fears at Bay?

BY CHRIS, A WISE WOMAN I MET ON THE JOURNEY

I remind myself:

I am a child of the universe, no less than the trees and the stars; I have a right to be here. And whether or not it is clear to me, no doubt the universe is unfolding as it should. I am a beautiful prism of rainbow colors, pink and yellow and blue and lavender and peach and mint green. I am only housed in this body of scars. I am here to learn deeper meaning, and without this body I would have a much harder time learning what I need to. My children are strong and beautiful and good, in some small way because of who I am and how I mothered them. When I see what wonderful and wise parents and lovers and spouses and friends they have become, I need to remember that they got some of that from me.

I have been very fortunate to have walked through the valley of the shadow of death, and more than one time. I keep coming back because there is love here, and warmth and goodwill.

Although humans can sometimes be cruel, there are not many who would willingly hurt another soul. It is the paranoia run rampant in our society that tells us to fear one another. We can live in the faith and knowledge that we all are truly one, individual parts of the whole.

I curl up in my little house, wrapped up in a ragged pink blanket that I have had for thirty years. I eat chicken noodle soup (the cheap Campbell's kind). And I sleep. I am usually able to calm myself with the conviction that when I am rested, I am better able to deal with fear.

I make lists: pros and cons, decisions or actions I can take.

I analyze. I drive around. Around and around.

I run on the treadmill. I go see a scary movie. (Fight fire with fire?)

I cry. And I pray. And I eat.

I take deep breaths, or sometimes, just remind myself TO BREATHE.

Within two pages, Chris says what I take a whole book to say: that fear disappears or is transformed when we remember and act from who we really are. I appreciate her willingness to share her wisdom, beauty, courage, and strength.

1
Recognizing Fear, or <u>F</u>ace Everything <u>A</u>nd <u>R</u>ecover[1]

If we live in a chronic state of fear, then fear becomes the base against which we compare every other experience, and we stop noticing that we are afraid. This makes it difficult to recognize and fully experience the fear, which allows it to move through and out of our bodies; it also makes it hard to fully appreciate any other states, such as joy. These exercises are designed to help you recognize and experience your internal and external states of being, be they fear or anything else.

EXERCISES FOR PAYING ATTENTION

We often live our lives unconsciously, habitually, not really paying attention to what is happening around or within us. These three exercises are designed to help you wake up to your own life. Although this book is primarily focused on recognizing and transforming fear, it is important in these first exercises not to go into them with the assumption that all you will find is fear. Research shows that we assign different feelings to the same internal experience depending on the situation in which we find ourselves. Thus, the same internal experience might be interpreted as fear or excitement, depending on the other cues that are available. I encourage you to simply notice your internal experience without immediately attaching a label to it.

■ Exercise 1.1A: Paying Attention to Breath

Begin by observing your breath and noticing where and how it moves (or doesn't move) through your body; notice where it flows freely and where it gets stuck, and any additional nuances. You can even imagine seeing the breath as it leaves the lungs and enters the bloodstream, going to all of the organs and eventually down to the cells. In this way the breath moves throughout the entire body.

■ Exercise 1.1B: Paying Attention to Movement

Go for a meditative walk and observe your body just like you observed your breath: how it moves, where it feels free-flowing, and where and how it feels restricted or constricted. Although there are specific instructions for some types of walking meditation, I recommend that you slow your walk and become conscious of what is within you. If you feel as though you need structure, try clasping your hands together in front of your belly (this will help you remember to belly breathe during the meditation; see Exercise 3.3 for help), shortening your stride, and slowing your pace by making sure that the front foot is completely flat before lifting the back foot, heel first. You may find that walking a labyrinth[2] is helpful in this practice, as the twists and turns require a slower pace and focused mind.

■ Exercise 1.1C: Paying Attention to Daily Life

Notice where in your everyday life you stop short, hold back, or choose not to go; the thoughts you won't allow yourself to have, the feelings you won't acknowledge, the spiritual practices you don't follow through with, the person you can't face, the choices you don't make, the direction you won't go. Ask yourself, Is this the choice of a person who loves life, or of one who fears life?

EXERCISES FOR PAYING ATTENTION TO BELIEFS

One of the areas of our lives where we tend to be most unconscious and most fearful is in the area of beliefs, or the "rules" by which we live our lives. These beliefs can be personal, familial, cultural, or even religious. Fear often arises whenever we go against these internal rules. The following exercises are meant to help you become aware of your unconscious beliefs and decide whether or not you want to continue to live your life this way.

Though some of these beliefs may seem very generic while others are more specific to issues of health and wellness, all of them may affect how we approach the processes of staying well or of healing. For instance, one of your family rules may have been "Others always come first." You may have watched your mother serve everyone at the dinner table before she finally sat down to eat. But you may be applying this to your own life in ways that ultimately damage your health. Perhaps you are sick with a cold but insist on taking the second-grade Sunday-school class sledding as you promised, and the cold turns into pneumonia. Be sure to identify the places where your beliefs could be negatively or positively affecting your well-being.

■ Exercise 1.2A: Paying Attention to Personal Beliefs

Go back to what you noticed in the first three exercises. Allow yourself to play with what of belief might be at work in anything you discovered about yourself. These beliefs might be especially easy to access when you remember the very first time you were stopped or stopped yourself from acting a particular way; they might also have developed out of scary or dangerous situations. Some examples of these beliefs are:

1. You notice that you don't breathe very deeply, and that your breath tends to stay up around your throat. You remember that your coach or drill sergeant told you to suck in your stomach; even though it didn't feel good to do that, you decided that life would be "safer" if you did what you were told.

2. As you walk, you notice that your arms don't swing, while those of other people do. You experiment with this, and notice that you feel a little anxious when you allow your body more freedom. You might wonder if you have unconsciously developed a belief that you shouldn't take up too much space because you don't deserve it or because it's not fair to others.

3. After suffering an injury from a bike accident you decide that riding a bike is too dangerous and you permanently loan your bike to your sister or a friend. Years later someone suggests going on a bike trip and you say, "Oh, I really don't like bike riding."

■ **Exercise 1.2B: Paying Attention to Familial Beliefs**

Though we obviously create our own beliefs, many of these beliefs are taken unconsciously and without question from our families. Familial beliefs often go back several generations. Take some time to observe your family's various behavioral, emotional, and spiritual constrictions, which often turn into what might be called a family motto. These usually begin like this: "Our family always . . ." or "My family never. . . ." Play around with this; think about the kinds of beliefs that might underscore your family mottoes and behavior patterns. For instance, a family in which someone was sent to prison for beating up a person in a fit of rage might develop the motto (and appropriate accompanying behaviors) "No one in our family ever gets angry."

Family Birth Order and Beliefs

Your birth order—your chronological position in your family, whether only child or oldest, middle, or youngest—may account for some of your beliefs and behavioral patterns. Psychologists who have studied this have come up with some characteristics that seem to hold up across families. Firstborns, (an only child classifies as a firstborn) tend to be high achievers, working harder for grades, jobs, and so forth than those born after them. They also tend to be perfectionistic, overly responsible, and focused on rules. Middle children are often known as the "peacemakers"; as the ones in the middle they manage situations by being diplomatic and social. Last borns are often the most rebellious and likely to take risks.[3]

Pat, a psychologist, told me how her family position affected her experience of school: "I was afraid I wouldn't do well. I'm a first and only child, and I had lots of messages about doing well and 'weller.'" It makes sense that birth order characteristics are shaped by our families—by our parents' hopes and expectations, our own needs to please them, and the natural competition that arises with our siblings. As the oldest, we might fear loss of parental affection; as the youngest, we might feel that we have to do something outrageous just to get noticed. These same forces come into play in other situations as well. For example, if we aren't the perfect patient, perhaps the doctor won't give us as much of his or her time; if we don't kick up a fuss, we won't be noticed by the nurse who is clearly overworked.

You can even gather ideas about absent family members or ancestors by listening carefully to family gossip and history. Or try "dialoguing" (see Appendix B for additional information) with one of these people by using a well-known Gestalt therapy technique called the "empty chair." Sit down opposite an empty chair. Imagine that one of your least-known family members is sitting in that chair, and ask him or her questions about his or her beliefs. Relax, and allow your imagination to supply the answers, as though they were coming from that person. You might want to do this out loud with a tape recorder running or have someone there who can take notes for you. Quite often the unconscious is aware of things that the conscious mind is not, and the answers will more easily appear in this way.

I recently heard a wonderful story that illustrates how we unconsciously take on familial behaviors. When it came time for a newly married woman to prepare her first Easter dinner, she went out, got a ham, brought it home, cut off each end, put it in a pan in the oven, and roasted it. When her husband saw the cooked ham, he asked what happened to the ends. The woman explained that she had always seen her mother prepare ham that way. The next day she called her mother and asked about the ham, and her mother said, "Well, that's the way your grandmother always did it." So the woman called and asked her grandmother, who replied, "Oh, that's the only way it would fit in my pan."

■ **Exercise 1.2C: Paying Attention to Cultural Beliefs**

Beliefs can also come from our ethnic and cultural heritages, sometimes going back centuries. These beliefs can be accessed by reading the myths and fairy tales of our ancestors; they have a lot to teach us about ourselves, what it is to be human, and how to deal with basic human issues such as fear. On the following pages I have included the story of Iron John, a fairy tale that I believe can teach us a lot about fear. Since it is Germanic in origin, it probably speaks better to those of us who are of Northern

The Influence of Culture on Our Experience of Fear

Barb, a post–breast cancer thriver and activist, has some interesting observations about her cultural "family": "There is a whole culture of fear amongst Jews; generations' worth. It's in our cells. This perspective affects how you look at your body, the world, healing. For Jews, worry is a big theme. You often see things negatively; you're often ultra-sensitive. A lot of power in America has been given to the medical establishment, so our role as victims becomes ever more profound. My grandmother, who is still alive and in her nineties, would do anything a doctor told her to do without question."

Ellie is a lawyer who works in the public health field. Part of her job is to get certain public health policy messages out to the various communities for which she is responsible. She realized that the Mexican community was not following through on a message that had to do with the various inoculations required for school-bound children. When she went out and talked with people in that community, she was told that because of their culture, which often disregards subtle ads, the ads her agency sponsored needed to be more dramatic—to the point of being "hysterical" (that is, fear-inducing)—in order to get the attention of the parents.

European heritage. If any of your ancestors come from a place other than Northern Europe, you might want to do some additional reading within that culture's mythology, looking for stories that tell you about how that culture perceives and deals with fear. The story of Buddha meeting the highwayman on the road, for example, is another such story. Still, Iron John is a good place to begin; simply read the story to yourself or have someone read it to you and see if you resonate with any portions of the story.

MYTHOLOGY: A LOST SOURCE OF KNOWLEDGE

As you read the story of Iron John, stay connected to your belly through your breath. Pay attention to where you first enter into the story on a personal basis—that is, where do you get hooked? At what point do your emotions get called into play? What are they? Does fear ever show up? With which characters do you identify? At what point would you be frustrated if you weren't allowed to continue the story? There are additional questions in the next exercise, a visualization in Exercise 5.4, and an interpretation of the story in Appendix A. Please do not read the interpretation until after you have explored the story completely for yourself. Myths and fairy tales are much like dreams; though there are universal or collective aspects to them, each person's perception of them is colored by his or her own life experiences. My interpretation reflects who I am and may have little to do with how you experience the story.

As with many myths and fairy tales, the main figures in this story are male. The women—a queen and a princess—appear in the background. There are several theories about why this is so, but the one that may be most useful in approaching this story is the idea of archetypes, which was first described by Carl Jung.[4] An archetype is a "psychic structure" that is thought to be common to all humans. Thus, we all have interior kings and queens, wild men and witches. In general, male aspects are considered to reflect our more active natures, while female aspects are thought of as more receptive. At the same time, there are both active and passive ways of receiving. Think about the difference between two friends, one of whom listens intently as you speak, and can then respond in a deep manner and one who is listening with only one ear and then vaguely responds to your needs. Keep these ideas in mind as you read the story.

———————————■———————————

Iron John: A Story about Fear

Once upon a time there lived a king whose castle was right next to a forest full of birds and deer and many other living creatures. One day a hunter went into the forest after a deer and did not return. Day after day, the king sent more and more men into the forest to search for the hunter, and none of them returned. Even their dogs did not return. Eventually, no one went into the forest anymore, and the king posted a notice warning people to stay away.

One day a stranger came along and asked the king for employment, offering to go into the forest after game. The king did not consent, explaining the dangers. But the man said, "I'll go at my own risk; I don't know the meaning of fear," and he went into the forest with his dog. The dog ran ahead and stopped at the edge of a pool. A hairy arm rose up out of the pool, grabbed the dog, and pulled him under. The man ran back to the castle, asking for the assistance of some other men to help him drain the pool. When the pool was drained, the hunter discovered a wild, hairy man at the bottom. He brought the man, called Iron John, to the king, who locked him in a cage in the courtyard, forbidding any-one to open the cage on penalty of death. He then gave the key to his wife for safekeeping.

Shortly after Iron John's arrival, the eight-year-old prince was playing in the courtyard, bouncing a golden ball, which ended up rolling into Iron John's cage. Iron John said he would only give the ball back if the boy released him from the cage. The boy refused, saying the king had forbidden it. When the prince asked for the ball on the third day, his father was out hunting. Once again Iron John asked for the key. The boy protested, "Even if I wanted to, I couldn't because I don't have it."

"It's under your mother's pillow," the wild man told him. The boy, who dearly wanted his ball back, retrieved the key and opened the cage door. The wild man stepped out, handed the boy his ball, and began to run away. The boy suddenly became afraid and yelled after Iron John, "Oh, Wild Man, don't go away, for I will surely get a beating." Iron John returned, scooped up the boy, and took him into the forest with him. When the royal couple returned to the castle and figured out what had happened, they fell into a period of deep mourning.

Once inside the forest Iron John informed the boy that if he did everything he was told, he would be fine, for the wild man had plenty of treasures and gold. The boy was asked to protect a golden spring; he was told to let nothing fall into it that would pollute it. Three times the boy allowed part of his own body to fall into the water; the third time it was his entire head of hair. Because of his failure, the boy was forced to leave the safety of the woods and go out into the world on his own. However, if he ever found himself in trouble, he was instructed to go to the edge of the forest and call Iron John's name, and the wild man would immediately appear to help.

With a hat to cover his golden hair, the boy went out into the world to look for a job, though he hadn't been trained for one. Eventually he found himself in another kingdom, at a palace where they took a liking to him and hired him to carry wood and water and sweep ashes. For the most part he managed to keep his hair hidden under his cap, but the princess discovered his secret.

The kingdom soon went to war, and when the boy asked to go with the soldiers they laughed at him. Once they had left, the boy went to the edge of the woods and called for Iron John, who gave him a steed and a troop of knights so that he was able to fight the king's enemies without giving himself away. The king then proclaimed a great festival that would last for three days and asked his daughter to throw out a golden apple to the knights each day. Again, with the help of Iron John, the prince caught the apple and rode away. Three days in a row he did this, but on the third day his headgear fell off and everyone saw his golden hair. When the princess revealed his identity to the rest of the court, the grateful king offered him whatever he wanted. The boy asked for the princess's hand in marriage.

At the wedding feast, the boy was reunited with his parents, who had never expected to see him again. A stranger also appeared, a proud king who announced himself as Iron John; he had been released from a magic spell by the prince's deeds. He offered the boy all of his many treasures.

———————◼———————

What does this story have to do with fear and health? In Appendix A I offer my thoughts on the topic, but again, before you turn there I encourage you to think about it for yourself, using the questions provided in the next exercise or some of your own. One way of thinking about such stories is to respond to them as you would a dream, viewing each of the characters as an aspect of yourself.

◼ **Exercise 1.3: Journaling, Part I**

After reading or listening to the story of Iron John, answer the questions below. Refer back to the story and the questions on a regular basis as you work your way through this book, and notice how your relationship to fear changes as you work with it.

1. Where did you get hooked? At what point did your emotions get called into play? What were they?

2. Did you experience fear? At what point(s) in the story did it appear?

3. Did you identify with any of the characters? Which ones? Why?

4. Who or what is Iron John? Do you have your own Iron John inside you?

5. How did your Iron John originally come into creation? (Remember, he was originally a king.)

6. What does the golden ball represent? What is *your* golden ball? Have you ever lost it? When and how?

7. Why is it necessary for the ball to go into the cage? What if it never had?

8. How did you respond when the boy let Iron John out of the cage? What is being let out?

9. When has Iron John been let out in your life? If he hasn't been let out yet, what would prompt you to let him out? What would happen if you did?

10. What would transform your Iron John back into the king he truly is?

11. How does the existence of your Iron John affect your health?

12. Write about anything else this story evokes for you on the topic of fear.

■ **Exercise 1.4: Breathing into Places of Blockage, Stagnation, Pain, and Fear**

This is a follow-up to the previous exercises. Begin by breathing into the places in your body, life, or beliefs where you have identified some blockage, limitation, or fear. At the same time ask yourself, What is this about? Be open to receiving whatever information presents itself, in whatever fashion it comes. You may actually "hear" an answer in your mind, you might "see" an answer as a color or image, you might "feel" an answer as a sensation in your body. Take what you get and don't worry about interpreting it any further.

One way we stop ourselves from knowing is by thinking within a certain box and throwing out anything that doesn't fit. For example, I once had a pain in my right shoulder, and when I asked for a healing image I got a panther. If I had decided "that doesn't make sense" and then suppressed the image, I never would have followed that image any farther; later, I saw that the panther had been shot in its right shoulder. My pain spontaneously disappeared when I discovered this.

SUMMARY

The exercises in this chapter are meant to help you recognize your fears. Perhaps along the way you have come up with some other exercises to help you. The next step in the process is to stay mindful of the fact that you carry fear with you; the next set of exercises will help you to do that. Or maybe the mere act of recognizing your fears has begun to chase them away. See chapter 3 for more assistance with releasing your fears.

2
Reporting and Acknowledging Fear

If you are experiencing fear, the next step is to admit it to yourself and others. Fear gains strength from secrecy: if you don't acknowledge your fears they can run rampant in your psyche; and if you don't talk openly about your fears, you may imagine that they are yours alone, making the experience even more intense, weighty, and frightening. The following exercises are designed to help you acknowledge your fears.

■ **Exercise 2.1: Journaling, Part II**

Continue to write about what you discovered in the first chapter's exercises. Think about the times, places, situations, and people in your life that have evoked fear. Write about each experience as you think of it. This will be an ongoing process; return to this exercise whenever you have a new memory or experience of a fear-producing situation.

Although I use the word *write* when talking about journaling, I encourage you to think of it more broadly. Some of you will find that writing is the best medium for capturing your thoughts and feelings about fear, while others will find that drawing, painting, sculpting, collage, or even dance is preferable. The whole point of this exercise is to begin the process of moving your internal experience through and out of your body and mind, putting it into an external "container." This actually begins the process of release, which is the subject of the next chapter.

■ Extra Credit (preparation for Exercise 3.1B)

Each time you identify another fear, pick up a stone; this will represent that fear for you. Put all the stones in a pouch, and carry them around with you occasionally. Pay attention to how that extra weight feels—what it does to your body and your movement. How many stones does it take for you to notice the extra weight or mass? How many before the weight becomes a limiting force?

EXERCISES FOR SPEAKING THE FEAR ALOUD

It's one thing to acknowledge your fears to yourself, in the privacy of your mind, heart, or journal. It's quite another to speak them aloud, to give voice to them. This can actually begin the phase of releasing, as you physically move some of that energy out of you.

Many people choose during times of illness to become quiet and hide from themselves, their family, and their friends. This withdrawal may be due to a fear of burdening others, of making the illness more real, or of being deserted when they most need people. But now is a good time to take the risk of speaking out, to tell people what is going on with you and what all of your fears are. This is a tremendous gift you can offer to others—a chance to give to and support someone else.

■ Exercise 2.2A: Speaking the Fear Aloud to Yourself

Read aloud each fear you have written about in your journal, looking yourself in the eye in a mirror. Notice how it feels to do this.

Tell Me Your Story

Dee is the director of spiritual needs assessment in a community clinic's outreach program. Her job is to see that the spiritual aspect of a client's health care is being met. She acknowledges that there is a lot of fear within the system these days. Patients are fearful of the unknown, of pain, and of being isolated; staff members are afraid of doing or saying something wrong in patient care and then being called on it; doctors are wary of intimacy with their patients; they are also afraid of not having control as physicians because of HMO involvement.

"The biggest antidote to the fear is, primarily, communication," says Dee, "and the biggest problem is the lack of communication."

There are many reasons for faulty communication. Because of the discontinuity of staff, no one feels responsible for any given aspect of a patient's well-being. Further, information is often seen as "a privilege, a resource for the elite few." Patients sense this and begin fearing that their doctors are withholding vital information from them.

Dee also sees creating personal relationships as an antidote to fear. In her outreach work she combines communication and a personal manner to help ease the minds of patients. She explains, "I begin my visits by asking the client or patient, 'Tell me your story.' First I get the story of the illness, then the family history, and finally I hear about them. Very often their first response is, 'There's nothing special about me,' and then I get these incredible stories. Usually they end by thanking me." Who among us wouldn't be grateful for having someone take that kind of personal interest in us and our feelings, especially the emotions that scare us?

Is it easy or difficult? Is it more difficult to name your fear or to look yourself in the eye? A lot of people have trouble with the latter; it gets easier with practice. Remember to journal about this.

■ Exercise 2.2B: Speaking the Fear Aloud to a Trusted Friend

Read aloud each fear you have written about in your journal to a friend or someone else you trust, such as a priest, minister, or rabbi. Having an ally in the process of dealing with fear is very powerful. (See also Exercises 4.9A and B.) Note in your journal how it feels to share your fears.

■ Exercise 2.2C: Speaking the Fear Aloud to a Group

Read aloud each fear you have written about in your journal in front of a group. It can be a group of friends, a therapy group, a spirituality group, an Emotions Anonymous group, an AA group, a hospital support group for patients or family members, and so forth. If it is powerful to have one person on your side, think of how supported you will feel by a whole group of people.

> *The support groups allow you to bond with some other people; they give you a fresh perspective; they are healing.*
>
> —DOUG, HUSBAND OF SUSAN, WHO DIED OF CANCER

Choose a safe group in which to do this, starting with people who all agree to try the exercise. Begin by writing or typing your fears on sheets of paper, and then fold the papers and place them in a special bowl or some other container. Make sure that everyone in the group writes on at least one sheet. Mix the papers and pass the container around the room. Each person should take out one paper, then read aloud the fears that are named on it. This allows the fears to be spoken aloud while the people are able to retain some anonymity. It also allows people to see that they are not the only ones who are afraid; in fact, quite often they will find their exact fears verbalized by someone else. This can be an extremely liberating experience.

■ Exercise 2.3: Honoring Fear

Though its purpose has been twisted, the original function of the fear was to help the body deal with something the psyche considered dangerous through fighting or engaging or fleeing. But fleeing, avoiding, and denying do not help health; a more proactive stance is required.

If, as Arnold Mindell maintains, our illnesses are our greatest dreams trying to come true,[1] perhaps these dreams and our fears about them should be honored rather than avoided. Take a few minutes to think about your fears of your physical symptoms or illness and what they might mean from this perspective. Ask yourself, How has this illness or fear changed my direction in life? What has it pointed me toward? What has it guided me away from? What have I chosen to fight harder for? What have I let go, realizing that it really wasn't all that important to me? For what can I give thanks to this illness? For what can I give thanks to the fear?

> *Perhaps everything that frightens us is, in its deepest essence, something helpless that wants our love.*
>
> —RAINER MARIA RILKE, *LETTERS TO A YOUNG POET*
>
> ■
>
> *Fear was an ally, trying to point me in a different direction.*
>
> —CARI, A FORMER DANCER

Imagine yourself honoring the fear in some way, like shaking its hand and thanking it for a job well done, or dialoguing with it (see Appendix B); this acknowledges the original intention of the fear and can clear the way for its release.

SUMMARY

Having reported your fears, you have already begun the process of releasing them.

3
Releasing Fear

You may have already begun the process of release just by acknowledging the fear. Now you will consciously and actively focus your attention and intentions on this part of the process.

Having a trained bodyworker use pressure-point massage to release the fear that is stored in various places in the body can be extremely beneficial, but it may seem like an expensive luxury. Some bodywork techniques can be self-practiced on your own body, or a friend can help; courses such as self- or partner-shiatsu, for instance, are available in many locations. Some of the body-oriented psychotherapies, such as Hakomi or Arnold Mindell's "process work," are similarly effective and adaptable to self-work.[1]

It is important to remember that as the fear is released it will stir up all kinds of feelings, images, and body sensations. Thinking of these sensations as the release of toxins from the body may help you through. As anyone who has completed a detoxification program can attest, you often feel worse before you start feeling better. Since the process may include some dark emotions, it may be useful to do the work with an ally who can be present to witness the fear and remind you through constant touch or verbal reassurances that you are totally safe. Having your ally hold your feet or ankles gently but firmly is a wonderfully simple yet safe and grounding kind of touch.

EXERCISES FOR LETTING FEAR MOVE
THROUGH YOUR BODY LIKE A WAVE

Fear and other feelings are meant to flow through the body and mind quickly and easily like a wave, but we often interfere with this process by getting caught up in the feelings. These exercises facilitate the release of fears that have been trapped or held.

■ Exercise 3.1A: Letting Fear Move Through Your Body as a Sensation

This exercise builds on Exercises 1.1A and B. As you notice the sensations and stagnant places in your body, be aware of any movement, no matter how small. As sensations begin to travel around within your body, follow them wherever they lead, imagining them as waves moving through the body. Allow them to appear and disappear naturally, perhaps flowing right out of your feet or fingertips or out of the top of your head.

■ Exercise 3.1B: Letting Fear Move Through Your Body with Physical Assistance

Although this exercise is specifically for people who had difficulty with Exercise 3.1A, it is a fun exercise that can be beneficial for anyone. This exercise is best practiced outside near a body of water—moving water is especially appropriate.

Take the stones you collected in the Extra Credit portion of Exercise 2.1. Using either hand, grasp one of the stones and hold it near your belly. Choose one of the fears on your list and say aloud, "I release my fear of (name of fear)." Draw your hand up and across your body, releasing the stone into the water as your hand approaches its highest point. The physical movement should feel something like a wave. You can add to the experience by imagining an internal wave moving up from your belly, out your fingertips, and away from you with the released stone.

I recommend experimenting with the weight of the stones and the feeling they provide. Some people may find that lighter stones feel better, while for others the heavier stones promote the best experience. There may be a tendency to discount the value of this exercise; you might find yourself thinking, "This can never work" or "I've carried the weight of this fear around for too long to simply let it go like this." If thoughts like these surface, I encourage you to think of them as more of the fear and return to Exercise 2.1.

■ Extra Credit

Before leaving the water, or perhaps on your way back home, pick up one new stone that speaks to you of this releasing experience. Take home the stone and set it in a special, sacred place—such as on an altar—where it will remind you daily of the release. Each time you look at the stone, allow your body and mind to return to this place of peace and emptiness—a space that is ready to be filled with something new.

■ Exercise 3.2: Kidney Healing Sounds

In traditional Chinese medicine fear rules the kidneys, which means they are a main storage point for fear. Breathing into them, especially while practicing special verbalizations, is considered potent medicine for releasing the fear or any other blockage. In this exercise I offer a technique adapted from my studies with Ken Cohen, an acknowledged master of Qigong, an ancient practice for personal energy management. Another source for this type of work is the writing of Mantak Chia, a master of Tai Chi and Taoist healing practices.

Begin with your feet shoulder-width apart, knees slightly bent, with the backs of your hands resting on your kidneys (just below the rib cage on either side of the spine). Rub your hands back and forth over your kidneys three times. On the last rub draw your hands upward along the sides of your rib cage and under your armpits while saying, "Churee." Keep saying "Churee" in one breath as you slowly extend your hands and arms until they are in front of you, as though you were holding an immense ball between your hands and chest. Your hands should be at about shoulder height. Stop the verbalization before you run out of breath.

Repeat this exercise three times, then perform three harmonizing breaths as follows: Hold your hands at the level of your sternum, palms facing the chest, and elbows pointing straight out to the sides. Pull your elbows back as far as they can reach allowing the hands to follow. As you start to bring the elbows forward again, curl your hands into fists, bend forward at the waist at a forty-five-degree angle, and as your hands meet in the center roll them over each other three times, allowing that movement to originate in the shoulders, which roll in their sockets.

> *Fear is passion*
> *without breath*
>
> —DAWNA MARKOVA,
> *I WILL NOT DIE AN UNLIVED LIFE:*
> *RECLAIMING PURPOSE AND PASSION*

■ Exercise 3.3: Taking a Complete Breath: Belly Breathing

In Exercise 1.1A many people discover that their breathing never goes below their chests or even beyond the neck. This is usually because of anxiety, a "head" fear that takes place mostly in the realm of thoughts. By bringing your breath and consciousness deeper within your body, you are able to release this particular kind of fear quite easily.

The best way to ensure that you are making use of your entire lung capacity is to breathe all the way down into your belly, then into your midsection, expanding your rib cage in all directions, and then into the upper chest. To encourage proper technique place one hand on your stomach and the other on one side of your rib cage. As you inhale, the hand on your stomach should move

Breath Work in Childbirth

Leslie is a mother of two, a doula (professional birthing coach and assistant whose main purpose is to support the mother during labor and delivery), and a childbirth educator. "A lot of times I can pick out the people who are going to have difficult labors," she comments. "One of the ways I know they're going to have a tough time is the level of fear they bring into the class."

Generally, the women who are afraid are the ones who are less comfortable with and in their bodies, who can't comprehend how a baby can move through such a small place as the birth canal. "There's been a lot of documentation that anxiety and stress slow down labors, so I know that fear of childbirth has a big impact on women who have tough, slow labors that just don't progress. What helps women in labor is knowing how to relax, and having supportive partners."

Leslie also talks about the physiology of the fear response—the fight-or-flight response. "What will break the cycle, the escalation of fear, is muscular change," she says, noting the importance of physical movement. Obviously, birthing mothers can't go for a run around the block or do any kind of strenuous physical activity, but they can exercise the autonomic nervous system.

"The only way you do that is by breathing, because your breath sends the message to the brain that you don't need to fight or flee, you're really okay. It calms you down so that you break that autonomic cycle. I believe that's why breathing works in childbirth. There is a physiological reason why we teach breathing to people; it's not just to give them something to do."

forward. Once you have completely expanded your stomach with breath, begin to fill the midsection; your rib cage should expand beneath your hand. Feel the rib cage expanding in all directions, like a balloon, rather than in just two directions. When you have completely filled your midsection with breath, allow your upper chest to expand; your shoulders may even rise a bit. Hold the breath briefly, for two or three counts, then release in the opposite direction—first from your upper chest, allowing your shoulders to drop back into a relaxed position, then from your midsection, and then from your stomach. You should feel the hand on the stomach move in or back toward your spine. Practicing belly breathing for twenty minutes twice a day can work wonders,[2] but doing it whenever you think about it is also very helpful. Make sure you use this breathing technique while sitting in the waiting room of any clinic or hospital.

■ **Exercise 3.4: Expelling the Breath of Fear**

This is a variation on another exercise I learned from Ken Cohen. It is meant to expel toxicity from the body, such as fear that is stuck there.

Stand with your feet shoulder-width apart, knees slightly bent, arms relaxed at sides. Get in touch with your fear by breathing into your whole body, becoming aware of any fear or other stagnancy or blockages. Place your hands at the level of your sternum, palms facing your chest, elbows pointed straight out to the sides. Breathe in, drawing your elbows straight back, as if bringing them to touch behind you, and allow your hands to be drawn toward your armpits. As you exhale slowly, bring your hands to either side of your mouth, as if you were holding a ball in front of the mouth, and say "ho" from as deep in your belly as possible. Slowly bend your knees into a low squat, continuing to hold your hands at either side of your mouth and making the "ho" sound. When you have bent down as far as you can, swing your arms back behind you, pushing out the rest of your breath and along with it all the toxic fear that has collected in your body over the years. (You can add a visualization to this, such as seeing the toxins as a black cloud dispersing throughout the universe as you exhale.) As you come back up, slowly bring your hands and body to their starting positions, and once more breathe deep into your belly. Repeat the entire process nine times, ending with an exhalation.

■ **Exercise 3.5: Grief Work**

The same process that promotes fear prompts us to give up various aspects of ourselves. Once we begin this process we rarely stop; it just becomes easier and easier to give up parts of ourselves. (A wise eighteen-year-old girl I know once said, "I can't give in to my mother out of fear, because if I do it now I know I'll never stop.") When we begin to realize how much of ourselves we have given up or abandoned, we often experience grief. By acknowledging this grief and releasing it through tears, sobbing, wailing, the stamping of feet and other forms of expression, we continue making space for the return of our true natures. We also become less likely to abandon aspects of ourselves in the future.

Grief may also be a part of any illness that results in loss, whether it is temporary or permanent, physical or emotional. The same strategies for release apply to this type of grief.

EXERCISES FOR ANGER

After grief there is often anger at those who, wittingly or unwittingly, asked us to give up pieces of ourselves—for example, doctors and surgeons. We may also become angry at God for allowing it to happen, and at ourselves for abandoning our true natures. Many people want to skip over this step because they fear anger, whether in the form of reprisal from others or their own overwhelming, hard-to-control anger. But the safe expression of anger is an important step in transforming fear.

Excerpt from Tamara's Journal

The waves are spectacular today—great green foamy things. They strike the immovable rocks with all the fury I could ever hope to summon up to throw at whatever fate brought this cancer on me. Curious how much it helps me just watching this timeless dance between water and shore. The cancer and the chemicals in my body are dancing, too. Hopefully, unlike this rock, the rock-hard tumor in my left breast will be more easily dissolved by the water and chemicals washing against it.

■ Exercise 3.6A: Physical Expressions of Anger

Stomping your feet, hitting a pillow, scrubbing the bathroom floor until it shines, and breaking nondangerous items are all wonderful ways of releasing anger. Ellen Hufschmidt, a ritualist located in Minneapolis, has led anger workshops for years that involve the breaking of clay pots and the subsequent creation of something from the shards. This transforms the energy of anger. You can combine physical expressions of anger with the following exercises to put your unique stamp on it.

> *If you can't be fed, be bread.*
>
> —RUMI

■ Exercise 3.6B: Preverbal Expressions of Anger

Grunting, screaming, or vocalizing in unique ways gives additional expression to physical expressions of anger. Because the fear or concern of what others might think may constrict you in really letting loose, it's best to try this exercise alone at first. Begin by belly breathing (see Exercise 3.3), stay out of your head, and let the sounds come from way down deep.

■ Exercise 3.6C: Verbal Expressions of Anger

You can, of course, use actual words and phrases to give additional voice to your anger. Just be careful of getting too caught up in your head; pay attention to your gut and its need for expression of anger. You may choose to express yourself verbally in your journal. (See the sidebar Excerpt from Tamara's Journal on page 53.)

■ Exercise 3.7: Forgiveness

Once we have expressed anger, forgiveness is possible. Forgiveness is another method of releasing feelings, such as anger, that we have been holding on to. We may need to forgive ourselves for what we have given up, others who asked or forced us to give up those things, or even God. This process may require making amends, including with ourselves. A good mantra or affirmation for this process is, "I forgive everyone. I forgive myself. I forgive God. I forgive all past experience. I am free!"[3] To further facilitate forgiveness, you may want to recall a time when you felt forgiving or experienced forgiveness from someone else, then reconnect with that energetic experience as you repeat the affirmation.

EXERCISES FOR BEING HEARD

It's one thing to give voice to your fears, to say them aloud and begin the process of releasing them. It's quite another thing to feel heard—to have the experience of being understood and even empathized with. When you don't believe you are heard it often feels as if the fear you spoke aloud hit a brick wall and bounced right back to you. When I found the lump in my breast one of my worst fears was of not being seen and heard for who I truly was. Neither of the Western medical doctors I consulted was able to see and hear me as a unique individual with particular fears and certain beliefs and needs within the healing process.

Try Exercises 2.2B, and C again, ensuring that you feel heard. Only you can know if you have been heard. One way of determining this is by asking the person who is listening to you to repeat what she thinks you said. If she really heard you, she will be able to repeat what she heard, in her own words, in a way that lets you know she truly understood you. If she can't, keep dialoguing until you experience being fully received. Another way of determining whether or not you've been heard is by evaluating how you feel after speaking. You feel comfortable or "right" by what happens in your body.

Trying to be heard is often a difficult task under the best of circumstances, let alone at a time when we feel especially vulnerable and mortal. Therefore it might be best to practice these exercises in advance of any serious illness, simply as a part of your daily life.

■ Exercise 3.8A: Being Heard and Seen by Yourself

You may have been unwilling to look at or acknowledge the full depth of your fears, afraid that it might make the fear or the object of the fear more real. Use this opportunity to go as deep as possible, as though you were cleaning out the last of the pus from an infected wound. Imagine your thoughts and your consciousness are a saline solution pouring into the wound and washing it clean.

■ Exercise 3.8B: Being Heard and Seen by Family and Friends

Talk to your family and friends about your beliefs about illness and healing. Let them know how you approach this area of your life, and let them know how you would like them to respond to you, how you would like them to treat you or honor you in the event that you do develop a serious illness. This is very much like developing a living will, in which you have to enlist the assistance of family and friends. As you practice with more and more people you will get a sense of who will be your best allies (see Exercises 4.9A and B) and under which circumstances they will help. Some people may be able to see and hear all of who you are, while some might be able to do so only under certain circumstances. For example, I've noticed that some people are especially good with feelings, while others are better at helping with physical tasks.

■ **Exercise 3.8C: Being Heard and Seen by Physicians**

Start interviewing doctors, primarily internists or family physicians. Let them know who you are and your beliefs about health, illness, and treatment. Get to know them. Do they see and hear you for who you truly are? Would you really be able to partner with this person? Under which circumstances? Or would you become merely a "patient" of theirs, waiting "patiently" for their ideas, words of wisdom, and treatment plans, rather than being a part of the decision-making process? Keep interviewing until you find someone you feel really good about. Unfortunately, most health care plans can make this process challenging, but you may want to pay a little more out of pocket in order to find a doctor who really listens to you. Remember that just as we tend to forget who we are under extreme circumstances, our doctors might as well. A partnership forged under ideal conditions may be tested mightily if the situation becomes difficult, so be prepared to change in midstream if necessary. It might be beneficial to have a backup physician in mind.

■ **Exercise 3.9: Checking Out the Reality of the Situation**

When we are ill we often face the potential for some very real losses—physical, familial, social, work-related, and so on. Although the potential for loss is there, fear can still cause us to make mountains out of molehills, or start us climbing the mountain long before it is necessary. We start living out the worst-case scenario as though it were actually going to come true, as though it were already happening.[4]

There is a fine line between being prepared, such as having a "blizzard kit" in your car if you live in Minnesota in the winter, and being paranoid, such as having that same kit in your car if you live in Florida and you "just never know."

Sometimes it helps to assess the situation in the "clear light of day." After using some of the previous exercises and achieving some level of calm, it is useful to reexamine the situation and see if, in fact, you have misunderstood, misperceived, or overreacted to any aspect of it. Just like children can mistake objects and shadows in their rooms for the boogeyman, so can we exaggerate a situation.

For example, when many people hear a physician utter the word *cancer*, or even a more benign word like *tumor* or *growth*, they immediately imagine the worst and often fail to hear the rest of what the doctor has to say. Though this is sometimes the fault of the doctor—call it poor people skills or poor communication skills—it often has more to do with the listening skills of the patient. This is why allies, even in the form of a tape recorder, are very valuable when we consult with health care professionals. Allies allow us to go back through the experience, talk it over, call the doctor back, and look into alternative ways of perceiving the situation—which you may have missed because you were afraid.

> *Just because they're out to get you doesn't mean you're not paranoid.*
>
> —VARIATION ON THE WORDS OF AN OLD POSTER

SUMMARY

You have begun emptying out the fear, but do not expect this part of your work to be completed quickly. The problem is that as long as we are alive, living and breathing in a fear-based culture, fears will continue to be created or assumed. The best we can hope for is to stay as conscious as possible, willing to look at our fears directly rather than sweep them under the carpet. Hiding them works for a while, but eventually we trip over the mound that has been growing gradually. This is why the next phase, replacing, is so important.

4

Replacing the Fear with Something New

When you empty something, you create a vacuum. Nature abhors a vacuum, so it immediately seeks to fill the space with something. If you don't actively cultivate something new after you release a fear, or recollect the parts of yourself you previously cut out or off, the same old fear—perhaps in a slightly new guise—will most likely rush back in. But when we are happy with ourselves and our lives, when we are healthy and at peace, there is less reason and room for fear.

The following exercises are designed to help you remember who you really are so that you can cultivate something new to fill the void.

■ **Exercise 4.1A: Too Little Information**

By far, the number one answer to "What was helpful in releasing or transforming your fear as quickly as possible?" is "Information." (See the sidebars Information, Please on pages 60–63 and Bernadette's Story on pages 142–46.) Sometimes this means getting or demanding additional information from your medical doctors or finding new physicians who will talk more openly with you. Sometimes this means seeking out other resources, such as the Internet (see the Bibliography for some good Web site recommendations) or alternative healers. And sometimes it means going within and getting information intuitively. (See Exercise 5.5 on Dream Work for a way of finding information within.) The important point is to get as much of the information *you* need in order to feel informed and comfortable in making your treatment decisions.

> *Fear always springs from ignorance.*
>
> —Ralph Waldo Emerson

> *The most contagious disease we know is fear; a better response is to be informed.*
>
> —Jonathan Bain, MPR, Mid-Morning Show

If you have difficulty asking people, especially authority figures like doctors, for what you need, it often helps to practice this in advance. Make a list of exactly what information you need and the most likely sources for each listed item. Isolate the questions needing to be asked of physicians and prioritize them. That way, if you are given only a limited amount of time with a doctor, you will be clear about which questions to ask first. Then role-play your list of questions with a friend. Ask him or her to avoid giving direct answers. You might even practice asking for more time with the physician.

Exercise 4.1B: Too Much Information

On the other hand, sometimes we can be overloaded with information. Well-intentioned friends can often inundate people who have illnesses with advice, suggestions, and ideas—some of it bad, a lot of it good. But even the good information can become a burden; how do we sort through it all? Another seemingly unending source of information is the media. Every day there are new reports on medical discoveries and tragedies and countless ads about health care products, particularly drugs. What to do?

Information, Please

Here is what some people have to say about fear and its relationship to information:

Sarah: "I'm fairly well-educated and can sometimes use my research skills to get information for my friends that may help alleviate some of their fear. Sometimes it's information that their doctor should have given them!"

Leslie: "I think there are a lot of things that happen in the hospital that heighten your fear and that don't need to. For me, the biggest one is the withholding of information; you have to wait a long time for information to be given and that raises your anxiety, especially over a weekend. They would often do tests on Thursday and then we would have to wait until Monday. That always used to drive me insane, because I knew a lot of times the results were in on Saturday, but because our doctor wasn't on call we wouldn't hear about it until Monday. I remember one time pumping a resident for information because I knew that he knew the answer, and I finally got him to tell me. And then he made me promise not to tell the doctor that I knew.

"I would also feel less fearful if someone said, 'You know, we don't know what's going on here, so we're just going to try everything we know to figure it out,' rather than having them say, 'Well, we're thinking it could be a number of things, and we're going to do some tests for a number of things'—but they don't tell you what those 'number of things' are. I found out that I really had to probe."

Doug: "I'm coming from a place where expectations laid out in the treatment of ovarian cancer are not managed well.

The toxicity of the treatment was not laid out. Response rates, in the case of ovarian cancer, mean you're probably buying a matter of months of extended life, and the price of that is incredible toxicity, which they don't tell you.

"Susan carried a lot of hope, and there was no one that discouraged that, ever. Of course, they want to convey hope, but it's not ultimately a healing way to do it. Maybe they should have told us, 'You know, Susan, I think the toxicity here far outweighs the chances for success.'

"They would tell us at certain stages that something was life-threatening, but they didn't explain what that meant. One night Susan awoke with chills, but they subsided, so we went back to sleep. We didn't realize the significance of the chills—fever, infection, devastation—she nearly died that night by the time we figured it out. If only they had been more specific about what it means for something to be 'life-threatening. . . '"

Member of Modal Hospital team: "There are so many medical questions when you are first admitted. When the medical doctor wasn't there at the initial team meeting the patients and their families didn't get any medical information. Talk about fear—at your first meeting information can be very reassuring." (See Modal Hospital, pages 134–36).

Kathy (a psychotherapist): "As we processed [the hospital tests] afterward, my client's first complaint was, 'You know, nobody talked to me. Couldn't someone have gone over with me what was going to happen, what they were doing, why they were doing it? That would have helped a lot.'"

Kris: "I belong to an HMO. I recently noticed some lumps and bumps in my breasts and went to my clinic to have them checked out. I thought it sad that the medical staff showed their lack of knowledge or interest in the way nutrition relates to breast health. My surgeon referred me to a gynecologist who supposedly was an expert on diet relating to women's health. After meeting with her and hearing her say my guess was as good as hers, I started looking for information on my own.

"I know there is so much we can do as women to correct imbalances in estrogen with simple dietary changes. I gave up coffee and began taking vitamins C, E, and beta carotene, and a multivitamin and mineral supplement, along with changing to organic foods whenever possible, and I have noticed huge differences. My breasts are much smoother and are no longer sore prior to getting my period. Fear is born, I believe, in feeling out of control, so it is essential to learn what can be done to feel more in control and to lower your risks. Now that I have made these changes I do not fear finding lumps or whatever else comes along."

Diane (a nurse): "With many patients, questions need to be encouraged. They need to know that it's okay to ask questions, especially in such an intimidating environment as a hospital. In nursing school we are taught to look for clues to see if the patient understands and feels understood. I am not sure if a medical school curriculum emphasizes the same."

Often doctors themselves do not know the answers to their patients' questions. Many patients would rather hear "I don't know" than get a runaround; then they would know to look elsewhere for answers. In a world of such highly specialized medical disciplines, it's asking a lot to expect one person to be the sole source of information; this is why there are teams and second opinions and libraries. When in doubt, ask someone else, or find an ally who can help (see Exercises 4.9A and B).

For years, Andrew Weil, M.D., has recommended a once-a-week (or more) news blackout or boycott, during which we turn off the radio and the TV and don't read any newspapers or magazines.[1] Related studies have shown that women's self-esteem goes up dramatically when they quit reading "women's magazines." Our overall fear level may drop, thereby enhancing our immune systems, if we participate in a similar kind of information boycott.

I also recommend getting more proactive with friends. Tell them you'll let them know if and when you are ready for whatever information they might have, and then tell them what they can do for you, right now, that would be helpful. Perhaps one of them would be willing to become your personal "clearinghouse" for all the information, whether from friends, the media, or medical journals.

■ Exercise 4.2: Actively Seeking to Smooth out the Breath

In Exercise 1.1A you probably noticed lots of places where your breath was blocked or felt jerky. At that time you were just paying attention to your breath, but now you will actively engage in changing that breath to bring about a different kind of energy.

This can be done in several different ways. As you breathe (full-body or belly breaths), make the breaths as slow and gentle as possible, imagining that there is a feather in front of your nose or mouth that must not be disturbed. As you discover any rough places, find an image of smoothness you can use to help iron out the breath. You might picture the water's surface recovering from a pebble dropped into it or from the wake of a motorboat.

■ Exercise 4.3: Labeling the Fear as Something Else

In Exercises 1.1A, B, and C you were invited to explore your internal experience without labeling it. I mentioned that research has indicated the same internal experience can be labeled as either fear or excitement, depending on the person and the situation. In this exercise I invite you to reflect on a current situation that elicits fear and try out some other labels, such as excitement, anticipation, stimulation, passion, exhilaration, or fervor. Do any of them fit?

Often we have been taught to be afraid of such words and feelings (usually because a parent or teacher was afraid of them), which can account for our labeling of these experiences as frightening. For example, many of us were taught that being true to our inner selves, to our greatest hopes and desires, was too scary for those around us. More often, however, we have simply not had the opportunity to develop a large enough vocabulary to describe our experiences for ourselves.

■ Exercise 4.4: Talking Back to Fear

I have heard that fear is a monologue. But through dialoguing with ourselves (see Appendix B for additional information) we can change this dynamic and add some new ideas and energies to the equation. Look over your notes about your fear with an objective eye. Imagine that you are reading the journal of a loved one. What would you say to him or her? Make a list of your thoughts and comments, then weave them into a dialogue with the fearful part of yourself. Don't be afraid to get angry, passionate, or forceful; let the fear know that you are no longer afraid of it.

EXERCISES FOR GROUNDING

People in Western cultures tend to be cut off from the earth. Recent research proves that we are healthiest, happiest, and most at peace (not fearful) when we are connected to or vibrating at the same rate as the earth.[2] One of the easiest ways to achieve this connection is through grounding exercises.

■ **Exercise 4.5A: Walking**

The simplest way to ground yourself is to walk regularly and consciously on the earth, preferably in your bare feet. If you can't walk on the earth, imagine yourself walking on the earth as you walk through your daily life, or simply sit in a chair and imagine that your feet are planted on the bare ground.

■ **Exercise 4.5B: Whole-Body Breathing**

This form of grounding is also physical. Begin by belly breathing (see Exercise 3.3). With each inhalation, bend your knees and allow your upper body to lower toward the ground; keep your back straight. As you exhale, push your feet hard against the floor, imagining they are one with the earth (you might even imagine they are tree roots, extending down into the ground and drawing nourishment from the earth[3]). Allow your upper body to rise back up. Continue this exercise for several minutes. Although trembling in the legs may indicate undeveloped muscles, it is often a sign that energy is beginning to move.

The March Thawed Ground

*Some days I wake up
without fear,
wanting nothing
other than to sit here
with the snow melting
outside.
I am fond of the shy trees.
I am fond of my
dog's paws—
the toe tufts so immaculate
and seeming
to have been sheared
to flatter the shiny pads
and black nails.
Something keeps the fur
at such a length,
as it keeps the trees
just so tall.
And fear, if given up,
runs out so far and
melts into the March
thawed ground.*

—JERE, HUSBAND OF TAMARA

Dan's Bubble of Fear

Dan is a vice president for a major food producer. During his forties he developed a rare and powerful form of cancer. His story demonstrates the grounding, healing nature of touch. "My treatment involved radioactive iodine," he explains. "Everything in the room was covered with plastic. No one could come in and visit for more than fifteen minutes, and they had to stay seven to ten feet away. I was alone and afraid. I felt contaminated. The nuclear medicine people would come in with shields. There was no one to share my fear with. All outside connections were cut off. The fear was trapped inside the bubble with me; no one connected with it."

When Dan was able to move from his bubble to intensive care, he met what he refers to as "daisies," or people who create a "pocket of wellness in the system." He met more of them in intensive-care situations than anywhere else, probably because "you have to be a special person to survive there." Dan met two nurses whose presence he could "feel and was reassured by. They heard my fear when I couldn't talk. One would rub my forehead. I could feel the life source, the power [when she touched me]."

■ **Exercise 4.5C: Touch**

In my own story in the introduction, I relate how important it was for me to have an ally holding my ankles during a procedure with a surgeon. Valerie Hunt's work suggests that this experience is not unusual.[4] Just as synchronizing our vibrations with those of the earth helps to ground and heal us, so does synchronizing with another person; in fact, this personal connection seems to be one of the concomitants of the healings that Hunt studied. Though her work suggests that the synchronization of vibrations was intentional on the part of healers, it may also be an outgrowth of any experience of touch. (See the sidebar Dan's Bubble of Fear on page 66.)

■ Exercise 4.5D: Visualization

A fourth form of grounding can be done through visualization. While sitting or standing, imagine that your spinal cord extends from your neck all the way to the center of the earth. Allow the earth's energy to travel up the spine, mixing with your own energy. See the sidebar on pages 68–69 for an additional visualization on Grounding Your Energy.

EXERCISES FOR EMPOWERMENT:
FROM FEAR TO FIRE IN THE BELLY

In both traditional Chinese medicine and chakra theory, the belly is seen as a primary place where fear gets stuck or held. This is the place of creation, will, and self-esteem; it's no wonder, then, that fear disrupts our creativity and inhibits our actions. The next set of exercises is specifically aimed at replacing or transforming the fear in our bellies. Since we have bodies, we must pay attention to physical ways of empowering ourselves.

■ Exercise 4.6A: Sit-Ups or Roll-Ups

In terms of musculature the belly, the seat of the third chakra, is one of the least developed areas in the body. Doing sit-ups or roll-ups helps to strengthen this area, which is also known as the "powerhouse." Be sure to seek coaching from a fitness instructor on how best to do these exercises so that you don't injure yourself. There are also some great videotapes that focus on strengthening this area of the body.[5]

Guided Visualization:
Grounding Your Energy

This visualization exercise was created by Jere Truer, M.A., Lic. S.W. Please refer to Appendix C for general instructions for grounding and visualization exercises. See Appendix D for more information on the chakras.

Sit in an erect but comfortable position, with your feet flat on the floor and your hands in your lap. Close your eyes and take a few deep breaths. Let your whole body breathe, imagining that you are drawing your breath in, all the way to the tips of your fingers and toes. Notice your spine and how it supports your body. Imagine letting your spine descend from your tailbone through the chair down through the foundation of the building you are in. In this way, you are sending your "grounding cord" down from your first, or root, chakra at the base of your spine.

Open the first chakra and let the grounding cord plunge effortlessly down through the upper layers of the earth. Let it go down through the water tables, down through the crust of the earth, and down through a layer of granite. Let the grounding cord enter the first fire layer. Go through this layer into the conglomerate layer, through the conglomerate layer into the second fire layer, and through the second fire layer into the core of the earth. Ask the earth being to open its heart to you and receive you. If you wish, you may ask the earth how it is doing on this particular day, naming the day of the week and the date, including the year. The first time you do this, ask the earth to return all of the energy you have lost, repressed, or cast off in this life and in others. Ask that the energy be returned gradually over the next year. After you have done this once, you need not do it again.

Next, ask the earth to send its energy up to you. Receive the energy in your feet. Notice any subtle warmth or vibration. Let your feet be saturated with the energy, and bring it up through your ankles, calves, knees, thighs, and hips. Bring the earth energy into your first chakra and let it mix with your body's energy. Let the combined energies flow throughout your body. Bring the focus up to your second chakra or the area just below your navel. In your mind's eye, look around toward the back of the second chakra and tell any shadow or vestige of someone else's energy that it has to go. Watch it roll away. If necessary, pray for help. Now you are fully grounded and connected to the earth.

While remaining grounded, imagine there is a lotus blossom on the crown of your head. This is your seventh chakra, or head crown center. See the blossoms of the lotus open to the bright light above—the light of your soul. Let the light and warmth of your soul come down gently through the head crown center and into your mind and imagination. Open your third eye in the center of your forehead. Bring the light of your soul down behind your face, through your jaw, and down into the fifth chakra in your throat. Bring your soul down through your chest to the level of your heart, the fourth chakra. Guide yourself into the little home for the soul in the back of the heart, which is right next door to the little home for God. Now you are running your energy—connected with the earth and with God—through your soul. Notice that you are serving as a link between heaven and earth.

■ **Exercise 4.6B: Eating Well**

Poor nutrition saps our inner fire, but good food helps build the fire. While there are some general guidelines for eating well, there is no one way that works for everyone. In Asian medicine, for instance, there are numerous types of constitutions, each with preferred foods. My constitution doesn't react well to cold foods, especially in the winter, but this may not be the case for you. Interestingly, the blood type diet,[6] a more Western approach to individual eating plans that is based on blood type, has many overlaps with the Asian approach. In any case, you might begin with one of these approaches' recommended guidelines for healthy nutrition (see Weil's *8 Weeks to Optimun Health* or D'Adamo's *Eat Right 4 Your Type*) and then experiment with it until you achieve a diet which works well for you. One way to experiment is to take a small bite of something and see if your tongue likes the flavor. Then swallow the food and see if your stomach likes it as well. I can tell almost immediately after eating a small portion of some foods that it is best not to continue. Because of this, I have completely given up greasy fast foods.

Exercises for Balancing the Energy of the Third Chakra

You can have too little or too much energy in a chakra; either of these imbalances can cause a disruption in well-being. These exercises will help you balance your energy. (See Appendix D for a discussion of the chakras.)

■ **Exercise 4.7A: Taking Action to Balance the Third Chakra**

For people whose fear reveals itself as feelings of powerlessness that discourage the risk of taking action, one small act can create energy in this chakra. Begin by making a list of tasks or goals you want to accomplish, then break down each of those items into the smallest possible steps. Complete the first of those small steps and then congratulate yourself in some way. When you feel ready to go on, do the next step, again rewarding yourself in some way after you've finished. When one of the original tasks has been completed, do something extra special to celebrate.

■ Exercise 4.7B: Sitting Still to Balance the Third Chakra

For people who run around doing too much and often accomplishing little, meditating, sitting still, or taking a slow, purposeful meditative walk can help move the excess energy to areas of the body that need it more. Remember that frenetic movement is often just as fear-based as no movement; underneath is the fear that if you're not moving—physically or mentally—you are falling behind, being lazy, and so on. (If you haven't yet developed a meditation practice, see the Bibliography for the following references: *The Relaxation Response* by Herbert Benson and *Stress Without Distress* by Hans Selye.)

■ Exercise 4.8: Hara Breathing, or the Extended Belly Breath

The *hara* in Japanese (or the *tan t'ien* in Chinese) is an energy center inside the lower abdomen, a couple of inches below the navel.

Iona Marsaa Teeguarden, M.A., M.F.C.C., says, "The hara is like a sea of generative force and activity which gives us the ability to adapt to change."[7] Though I described simple belly breathing previously, I will now recommend a more structured approach.[8]

Stand with your feet shoulder-width apart and pointed forward, your knees slightly bent, and your arms hanging loose and comfortable at your sides. If standing is uncomfortable, you may sit in a chair; just make sure your spine is straight and your belly is not constricted. Inhale slowly through your nose to a count of five, making sure that you breathe all the way down into your hara, allowing the entire abdomen to expand. Hold your breath for a few seconds as you experience the breath and energy in your hara. Now relax, and gently exhale through your mouth to a count of five. Do not pause after the exhalation; instead immediately begin the next inhalation. Continue with this cycle for the duration of your meditation.

While fifteen or twenty minutes is a good length of time for this breathing exercise,[9] you will probably need to work up to it. In the beginning, five or even two minutes may seem like an eternity. Start with a time period that works for you and increase it daily or weekly until you reach the recommended length.

Anne's Story: The Need for an Ally

Anne had already suffered the fear, grief, and agony of a miscarriage when, two weeks shy of her due date, she visited the doctor for a regular prenatal appointment. Anne's belly was measured and determined to be a little small for the ninth month, so the doctor recommended an ultrasound. "That was fine," she recalls. "It didn't alarm me—they're pretty fun." The doctor also measured her amniotic fluid, which was quite low. Explaining why this could be a problem, he suggested that Anne see a specialist.

Though Anne usually went to these appointments with her husband, Michael, who was one of her allies, he couldn't get out of work that day so she had gone alone. The ultrasound was administered by a technician, whom Anne remembers as "nice but quiet. He wouldn't tell me much"—an occurrence that is by no means unusual since technicians are not authorized to share their opinions with patients. At this point Anne was still not worried or upset.

She continues, "Then the specialist came in. The first thing she said was, 'If I had things my way we'd deliver that baby right now!' It scared me. She insinuated that every moment this baby stayed in my womb was a threat to her life. It was so insensitive. I couldn't respond; I just listened, but I couldn't hear anything because I was in shock. I don't remember what she said after that point."

They hooked Anne up to a fetal monitor that beeps constantly as the rate of the baby's heartbeat changes. Although a nurse had explained what the numbers meant, she hadn't mentioned that the numbers tend to fluctuate. "She left, and . . . suddenly I am scared . . . thinking there's something incredibly wrong with the baby, because the numbers are going up and down, then staying flat for long periods of time. I'm also thinking it's my fault because I'm so upset. I sat there for what seemed like forever."

When a nurse finally came in to tell her she could go, Anne, seeking an ally, asked to speak to her regular doctor, who turned out to be unavailable. She then went to see her husband, and he too became upset. Once Anne got home her regular doctor called and calmed her down. She remarks, "He apologized for the other doctor frightening me, and explained that they [the other medical group] come from a totally different angle on health care. Their perspective is to get the baby out before something goes wrong, which is a fear-based medicine. They have all this technology and they want to use it, which means doing C-sections. That pissed me off."

Anne ended up not having a C-section. Her doctor told her the choice was hers, and she elected instead to be closely monitored for a week, during which she and the baby were just fine. At that point she decided to go in and be induced. "I wish I had waited another week, but it seemed too scary to wait and wonder if I was doing the right thing for another week. And it made sense, with the amniotic fluid dropping, to go ahead and be induced. My own doctor did recommend being induced after the one week. But [my daughter] wasn't ready to come out, hence my extremely long labor."

Anne's story demonstrates some of the difficulties with fear: it made her (and some of her practitioners) distrust herself and her body; it might actually have made the physical aspects (in this case, labor) more difficult; and it could have interfered with her trust in her own doctor. Her story also underscores the value of having even a single ally available to help you stay centered and trust in yourself and your own internal wisdom.

EXERCISES FOR WORKING WITH ALLIES

Research shows that having even one ally dramatically increases your willingness to trust yourself. The following exercises will help you develop a cadre of allies, both real and imaginary.

■ Exercise 4.9A: Working with a Real Ally

Choose a "fear buddy"—either someone who is committed to working on their own fear, or someone you trust to support you and give you truthful feedback about yourself and your work with fear. Ask your buddy to listen to you when you need a sounding board; ask her to go with you when you have to undertake something that is scary for you (such as a doctor's appointment or medical test); or ask her to give you suggestions and feedback when the task is something she can't do with you.

Julia's Team

When she was diagnosed with cancer, Julia knew she had some work to do to overcome the family mythology that anyone who gets cancer dies. She comments, "I did what I knew best, which was to start finding people who had succeeded. Being an athlete, my best bet was to find a team that I could work with and that would support me." Julia put together two teams—a real team of health care professionals, and an imaginary team of those who had successfully gotten through a similar journey, whose love and inspiration she took with her into any scary situation.

■ Exercise 4.9B: Working with an Imaginary Ally

This exercise should be done in conjunction with Exercise 4.9A. It is especially useful for situations when none of your real allies can be physically present with you. An imaginary ally can be a visualized version one of your real allies; it can also be a well-known figure from the present or history. Or it can be a fictional character who possesses some of the characteristics you would like to cultivate within yourself—such as fearlessness, courageousness, and centeredness—like the fearless hunter in the story of Iron John, or even an animal with some of those characteristics. (For example, bears are quite large and strong, foxes are often viewed as wily and living by their wits, and squirrels are industrious and prepare for their future needs.) Imagine that this person or character is part of you, perched on a shoulder or residing in your heart, and check in with him whenever you need support. Ask yourself or him what he would do in this situation.

An Ally on Your Shoulder

Leslie, the doula and childbirth educator we met previously, is also a business coach. She uses the following exercise with both her business clients and mothers-to-be; feel free to adapt it to your specific situation and needs.

Leslie tells her business clients, "See yourself as you are. Now identify a person in your life who has been an ally and role model for you—someone you think walks on water. Imagine that person sitting right there on your shoulder. Build up that image; imagine another supportive person right behind the first one, then another and another, until you can't think of any others. When you walk on stage to give a speech, you don't walk out by yourself; you're so wide you can't fit through the door because of all these people who are going out on stage with you, and will be there if you forget a line. These are the people who are going to say to you, 'Hey, that line is there somewhere; just relax and it will come to you.'"

To birthing mothers she says, "See yourself as you are. Now I want you to put your mother, your sister, your aunt, both grandmothers, your great-grandmothers, your great-great grandmothers, all the way back to the very first mother, on your shoulders. These are the women you came from; they have all been there, they have all experienced giving birth and are here with you while you're having your baby. You're just one in a long line of women who have successfully given birth."

Imaging allies is a technique that can be adapted to any general or medical situation. You may want to do some research to pull together a list of successful "mentors," as Julia did. (See the sidebar Julia's Team on page 75.)

Jere's Bear

Jere, a friend of mine, likes to tell a story that shows the potency of the imaginary ally. He was working in a halfway house in a rough neighborhood, and he invented a ten-foot bear as his ally. He took it to work with him every day, imagining that the bear was running interference for him, making sure no one accosted him. One holiday several months later, Jere left his bear at home because he expected the halfway house to be deserted and quite safe. As he entered he saw a house "regular," a Native American man, slumped over as if sleeping off a hangover. The man looked up, looked down, then up again, seemingly a little startled. As Jere passed him, the man asked, "Where's the bear?"[10]

■ Exercise 4.10: Creating and Using Touchstones or Talismans

A touchstone is a physical object—a stone, shell, ring, key, or shoe—or a word or image that serves as a reminder of who you really are. Any object that has meaning for you, like one of the stones you collected in the Extra Credit portion of Exercise 2.1, can work well. Don't, however, use a ring from a marriage in which you feel or felt powerless. Carry the talisman in your pocket or purse where it can be accessed at a moment's notice. The guided visualization in Exercise 4.11 is designed to help you both experience your power and transfer its energy to your touchstone so that merely touching it will bring you back to that sense of power. Since you will want to carry the talisman with you, especially when going to places or entering situations where you might expect to feel vulnerable, unsafe, or fearful (like a doctor's office, a meeting with your boss, or even surgery), you should choose an object that is small enough to fit in small places. New touchstones that are specific to a particular situation or need can be made at any time.

Patty's Sneakers

Diane, a nurse-midwife student, has a great story about one woman's unusual talisman.

Diane was working the night shift in the labor and delivery ward when a young pueblo woman, Patty, arrived alone by ambulance, already in labor. "While this delivery was her third," explains Diane, "she was still obviously frightened and shaken up." Diane postulated that the solitary ride and culture shock were major components of the woman's fear. While Diane hooked Patty up to a fetal monitor, another nurse began asking questions.

Diane continues, "When we discovered that this woman had not had any prenatal care, the nurse immediately became indignant. Under her breath, and in the presence of Patty, she would mutter such things as 'What is wrong with these women that don't get any prenatal care?' and 'How are we supposed to know how to take care of her, if she doesn't know when she got pregnant?'" The staff could not precisely determine the woman's due date, making it difficult to decide whether they should try to stop what might be a premature labor.

"It seemed to me that we as professionals could only cope with the situation by going on what we had in the present moment," Diane relates. "Chastising a woman who had not sought prenatal care and plaguing her with questions that she could not respond to was only going to augment her fear and self-doubt. Fear, self-doubt, and tension perpetuate not only pain but difficult deliveries as well. I recognized that our priority, for the welfare of this woman and her baby, was to diminish her fear and self-doubt, enable her to calm herself, and encourage her to breathe."

When Patty was moved to her own room, Diane asked to remain with her. "Once settled in her labor room, Patty began to calm a bit and tell me about herself." Diane asked Patty about her husband, her other children, and her life at the pueblo. The woman explained that she had been too scared to try to find any prenatal care. Furthermore, her mother, who had died within the last year, had been present at her first two births. Then she began to cry. Diane comforted her, and at the woman's request promised to remain with her throughout the birth.

Patty's sneakers also remained with her throughout the delivery. Diane recalls, "Those sneakers were her good luck charm, and she was determined to give birth while wearing them. At each juncture, from triage to the laboring room to her subsequent birth in the OR delivery room, everyone asked if she'd like to remove her sneakers—some more of a question, some more of a strong suggestion. She remained resolute in not removing her lucky sneakers. Even the OB/GYN had to smile at her sneakers propped up in stirrups on the OR birthing table."

By the time Patty was brought into the OR delivery

room, she was not the same fearful, confused patient that had first come to the hospital. She gave birth to a six-pound full-term baby who breathed spontaneously on her own, without any complications. "Both mom and baby were fine," Diane says, "after a successful vaginal birth by a woman who had regained her sense of self-confidence and calm focus after a frightening beginning."

It's obvious that several factors combined to help Patty transform her fear, not the least of which was Diane's receptiveness and calmness. But the best part of the story is Patty's tenacity in holding on to her sneakers, her talisman and the one object that connected her with her daily life and who she knew herself to be—despite being in the midst of the terrifying unfamiliarity of the hospital, with all its lights and technology and unfamiliar faces.

I usually advise people to use touchstones or talismans that can be hidden or that won't draw attention, but it's important to use something that will really work for you. If a stone in your pocket won't do, wear those sneakers or a purple hat or a Hawaiian shirt, and look for the smile it might spark on the unlikeliest of faces.

■ Exercise 4.11: Guided Visualization: Remembering Your Power

After adding fuel to the third chakra fire (see Exercises 4.6, 4.7, and 4.8 on eating and breathing) you are ready to explore its riches. I offer one way of doing this, but you might also come up with your own unique ways of exploring your personal power.

This exercise affords the opportunity for you to remember a time when you felt centered, strong, and powerful—not with power over someone else, but with the power to meet any and all of life's challenges—and to reconnect with that experience and refill yourself with that energy. It is also an opportunity to "charge" or increase the potency of your talisman (see Exercise 4.10 on creating a touchstone or talisman). After doing this exercise, even if your worst fears about your illness are realized, you will know—and your talisman will remind you— that you are not your illness, and you are not whatever you might have to give up as a result of your illness. You are, in fact, something much, much more—a powerful, complete being.

This exercise can also be revised slightly to focus on a time of total well-being and aliveness.

Refer to Appendix C for general instructions on grounding or visualization exercises.

While holding your talisman in one of your hands begin by connecting with your breath. Remember to take the breath deep into your belly. Take about two minutes for connecting with the breath.

As you continue to belly breathe, move your consciousness along with the breath down into your belly, into your power center. Notice how your power center looks and feels, including characteristics such as color, temperature, structure, tone, and quality. Perhaps it looks or feels like a warm, comfortable cave or womb, or perhaps it is more like a beach. It may be a strong fortress, it may look like a favorite place in nature, or it may look unlike any place you've ever been. In any case, it will have a sense of familiarity, as though you have finally come home. Stay with this for a few more breaths (about three to five minutes).

> *Our deepest fear is not that we are inadequate. Our deepest fear is that we are powerful beyond measure.*
>
> —MARIANNE WILLIAMSON,
> SPEAKER AND EDUCATOR

■

> *When we choose to think, believe, and act from a position of power, refusing to be a victim of circumstances, the healer within is automatically strengthened. When we refuse to live under the influence of worry and doubt, the internal medicine is enriched.*
>
> —RICHARD JAHNKE,
> *THE HEALER WITHIN*

From this power center, allow your consciousness to drift back to a time when you had the experience of being truly centered, grounded, and fully immersed in a feeling of personal power or total well-being—the sense that you, your body, and your soul were totally capable of meeting any challenge that came your way. If you have no memory of such a time, use an image from a movie or someone else's life—but put yourself into that image, imagining you are the hero or heroine, and claim it as yours.

It does not matter how far back in time you go to achieve this, but the clearer the image, the more potent it will be for you. Allow yourself to move fully into the image of you in that moment of power; wear it like a cloak. See and feel yourself in the image; be the image. Feel the power or the well-being coursing through your body, filling every muscle, every cell, every atom. Stay with this image for two to three minutes.

When you feel ready, bring this image and feeling of power forward in time to the present day. Remember your touchstone, and let it become a container for your experience of power. Pour all your experience of your own power or well-being into your touchstone until it's overflowing; notice that you do not empty in the process. Continue filling yourself and your touchstone for two to three minutes.

When you are ready, follow your breath back up and out into the world.

THE POWER OF VISUALIZATION

While growing up Karin had a long and difficult spell with medical problems. Between the ages of seven and nine, she would get dizzy and vomit daily; the problem slowly disappeared after the onset of puberty. She remembers fearing that the dizziness would hinder her dance career, but the true obstacle was the fact that one of her legs was shorter than the other. Surgery was considered, but the surgeon ultimately recommended against it. Karin's mother iterated, "Is this career really worth it?" Karin was both disappointed and relieved, since there would have been no guarantees with the surgery.

"What made me really afraid was my herniated disk," says Karin, a problem that developed in college. "At first, it was going to be a simple process of diagnosing and fixing it, but six months later it still hadn't been diagnosed correctly, and I was in a back brace. I stopped dancing and gained weight. I just did what they said because I trusted them and wanted to dance again. Fear put me on a crusade to find someone to heal me. I tried all kinds of chiropractors; I was even going to fly to Canada to have papaya enzyme dissolve the disk. At the last minute I didn't go because of a guy who ended up in a wheelchair from that procedure."

Eventually, Karin found a chiropractor who did help her. "At the first appointment he asked, 'Can you picture [visualize] yourself as healthy? I can't work with you unless you can.' I was really afraid—afraid I couldn't see myself as healthy and therefore wouldn't get well, or that I would do it wrong because I didn't know what that meant. Some part of me just did, and it worked, and five months later I was dancing again." Karin's story demonstrates the power of visualization, of belief in yourself (even when there's a part that doubts), and of the healing capacity of your own body.

EXERCISES FOR CULTIVATING HEART ENERGY

Research proves that fear, along with anger and sadness, depresses our immune systems, while love, appreciation, compassion, excitement, enthusiasm, support, caring, gratitude, and joy enhance the functioning of this system. It has also been said that love and fear cannot coexist. The heart chakra is considered to be the seat of love, the bridge between the lower and upper chakras (our bodies and spirits, earth and heaven), the connection between ourselves and others. The following exercises are meant to help you cultivate this bridging and nourishing heart energy.

■ **Exercise 4.12: Breathing into Your Heart**

Fear contracts the heart, closing it down. Breathing into the heart expands it, making space for new feelings and experiences. Before you begin, connect with your heart and notice its size and how it feels. Take about two minutes to consciously breathe into your heart, feeling it expand with each breath. Imagine it as a flower opening up. Now check in again with your heart. How has your experience of your heart changed?

■ **Exercise 4.13: Reaching Out and Drawing in Love, Joy, Compassion, Spirit, and God**

Our conscious intentions, choices, and actions have great power. By consciously choosing to draw certain energies to you, you become like a magnet for your own good. Drawing in love, joy, compassion, spirit, and God can counteract the fear, anxiety, or depression you might be feeling during a health care crisis.

This exercise should be done slowly. It can be practiced while standing, sitting, or lying down. Reach out in front of (or above) you, extending your arms, hands, and fingers and imagine you are reaching out for love—God's love, the universe's love, and so forth. Slowly draw that love energy in toward your heart until your hands come to rest on your chest. You can add words to this exercise, such as "I open myself to love (or joy, compassion, spirit, God). Love, come rest in my heart."

■ **Exercise 4.14: The Inner Smile**[11]

This is an exercise to practice ahead of time so that when you find yourself in a fear-producing situation you can more easily move through it. Imagine yourself in a current fear-producing situation. Concentrate on the feeling of fear; notice where it is in your body. Identify an earlier time or experience that was similar, perhaps the very first time you experienced that feeling. Smile into that part of your body. Allow the smile to expand from the one spot into every part of your body, filling every muscle, every cell, every atom. Allow the smile to expand forward in time, from your younger self to your present self. Now feel yourself radiating that smile out into the surrounding environment.

■ **Exercise 4.15: Remembering the Power of Your Love**

This exercise, which is similar to Exercise 4.11, recalls a time when you felt centered, strong, and powerful in the energy of love or joy or compassion, and helps you to refill yourself with that energy. It is also an opportunity to charge a physical touchstone with love (see Exercise 4.10 on creating a touchstone or talisman). For this exercise I recommend using a piece of rose quartz as your touchstone; this stone has long been connected with the heart and love. You might even be able to find a heart-shaped rose quartz.

Refer to Appendix C for general instructions for grounding and visualization exercises.

While holding the talisman in one of your hands, begin by connecting with your breath; remember to take the breath deep into your heart. Take about two minutes to do this.

As you continue to breathe into your heart, move your consciousness along with the breath down into your heart, into your center of love, joy, and compassion. Notice what your heart center

Loving Movement

Barb Wiener, who founded the Women's Cancer Resource Center of Minnesota, talks about movement in this way: "The time before diagnosis is the worst time, because once you have a diagnosis you have a task, something to deal with." But there are actions you can take before getting a diagnosis even becomes an issue. For some women, monthly breast exams help them to feel like they are involved in or even in control of their health. Wiener comments, "We need to be encouraged to know our bodies in a loving way, so as not to engender fear."

Physicians such as Susan Love and Christiane Northrup are picking up on this idea and suggesting that women approach their breasts in a loving manner, rather than making them the enemy. I once heard an interview with Dr. Northrup on National Public Radio in which she said, "If we examined our hands each month the way we examine our breasts, we'd have a big rash of hand cancer."

looks and feels like, including characteristics such as color, temperature, structure, tone, or quality. Just as there are many types of fear, so too are there many facets to the heart chakra. Explore yours. Stay with this for a few more breaths (about three to five minutes).

From this heart center, allow your consciousness to drift back to a time when you had the experience of being truly centered, grounded, and fully immersed in a feeling of love, joy, gratitude, or compassion. If you have no memory of such a time, use an image from a movie or someone else's life—but put yourself into that image, claiming it as yours.

It does not matter how far back in time you go, but the clearer the image, the more potent it will be for you. Allow yourself to move fully into the image of you in that moment of love; wear it like a cloak. See and feel yourself in the image; be the image. Feel the love coursing through your body, filling every muscle, every cell, every atom with your love. Work with this image for two to three minutes.

> *No one imposes fear upon us, rather we create it for ourselves in our own thoughts and emotions. What we need to realize is that we have just as much freedom to eliminate fear as we have in creating it.*
>
> —ERNEST HOLMES,
> *LIVING WITHOUT FEAR*

When you feel ready, bring this image and feeling of love, joy, and compassion forward in time to the present day. Remember your touchstone and let it become a container for your experience of love. Pour all your experience of your own love into your touchstone until it's overflowing; notice that you do not empty in the process. Continue filling yourself and your touchstone for two to three minutes.

When you are ready, follow your breath back up and out into the world.

■ **Exercise 4.16: Making Choices or Decisions from Love**

It is one thing to feel love when you are by yourself or engaged in a tender moment with someone you trust. It is quite another to act out of love when moving about in the world, engaging in a disagreement with a loved one, or facing a difficult decision regarding your health. Fear often enters into these interactions as we move to protect ourselves from some imagined danger. When faced with a decision in which you want to act from your heart chakra, use the rose quartz touchstone from Exercise 4.15 as a reminder of who you really are, and ask your heart what a loving, joyful, compassionate action would be. Be sure to thank your heart for its wisdom. It is important to remember that fear itself is often a choice that we make when love or another choice is not available to us.

■ Exercise 4.17: Developing an Attitude of Gratitude

Gregg Braden calls gratitude the lost mode of prayer.[12] In many ancient and recent spiritual texts gratitude is considered to be one of the most powerful modes of prayer. It certainly helps bring us back into the heart space. At the end of every day, make a list of all of the things for which you are grateful; include ongoing items such as family, health, abundance, and God's love, as well as events that happened that day. If you have trouble finding something for which to be grateful, remember that the gratitude does not need to be about something large or profound or personal; it just needs to be sincere. Some days the most profound gratitude might be for a sunset, the song of a cardinal waking you, or the taste of bacon on your tongue. Many sources also tell us that it is important to be grateful for things that seem not to have happened yet. The attitude of trusting that they are about to happen has a powerful impact upon us and the universe that supports us.

It's as easy as changing your mind.

JULIA, A WOMAN FROM ONE OF MY WORKSHOPS

■ Exercise 4.18: Making Friends with Your Treatment Choices

The treatments we choose will probably work better for us if we choose them out of love, appreciation, or gratitude for their help, rather than fear of what additional distress they might cause us or what might happen to us if we don't select them. I highly recommend that you take at least a day to consider how you feel about a doctor's treatment recommendation before acting on it. Make sure you ask the doctor about all the possible side effects or secondary effects of the drug or procedure, then take some time to reflect and meditate on this option. Is it really something you can embrace? Can you feel gratitude toward it for the help it may bring you? Or are you likely to feel coerced, resentful, at odds with it, or even fearful? What would it require for you to embrace this particular treatment option out of love or gratitude rather than fear? This process may include further discussions with your doctor, a second opinion, talking to someone else who has taken the same treatment path, or asking your dreams for help. If you cannot get to a place of love or gratitude, perhaps your psyche is telling you that this is not the best treatment choice for you at this time. Be patient, and let the knowledge come.

A friend of mine was very resistant to the notion of chemotherapy, with good reason—she had heard the same horror stories we all have heard. She finally accepted the chemicals into her body, but only after taking some time with each bag to bless it and visualize it helping her to heal.

SUMMARY

The process of working with and transforming fear will probably be lifelong. Fear is ubiquitous, tenacious, and habitual. But in having gotten this far you are beginning to bring more of your true self, your true nature, into the "habitual" realm.

5
Additional Exercises

These are advanced exercises that continue the work of previous exercises; familiarity with the earlier exercises will make these more accessible. If you have gotten to the point of working on these exercises, you are becoming a *responder*, a person who responds to rather than reacts to fear. You are now learning to express more of your true nature.

INDIVIDUAL WORK

■ Exercise 5.1: Qigong or Five Element Cleansing Meditation

This meditation does not directly address the issue of fear but helps us to achieve balance throughout our bodies. In Chinese Five Element Theory,[1] fear is associated with water, the kidneys, and winter; it is therefore released as we move into spring, which is associated with wood, the liver, and the emotion of anger.[2] In this philosophy anger is related to the energy that is needed for young shoots to push their way out of the ground and into the sunlight each spring. It may be useful to think of anger as the energy that counteracts fear, the water that has frozen (contracted) over the winter; this energy can melt the ice within you.

As with previous meditations and guided visualizations, you may wish to record this exercise or have someone read it to you. Take about two minutes to be with your breath.

We start with green wood, which is fed by blue water, and is associated with the liver. Begin by breathing normally. When you are ready, breathe the green energy of wood, of grass, and of trees into your liver through your nose. Exhale any used-up, impure energy through your slightly open mouth. Close your mouth, breathing the green wood energy into your liver. Open your mouth slightly and breathe out any impure energy. Repeat these steps for a few more breaths, then allow your breathing to return to normal.

Green wood becomes red fire, which is associated with the heart. When you are ready, breathe the red energy of fire, of the sun, into your heart through your nose. Exhale any used-up, impure energy through your slightly open mouth. Close your mouth, breathing the red fire energy into your heart. Open your mouth slightly and breathe out any impure energy. Repeat these steps for a few more breaths, then allow your breathing to return to normal.

From fire comes yellow earth, which is associated with the spleen. When you are ready, breathe the yellow energy of earth, of the sand, and of sunflowers into your spleen through your nose. Exhale any used-up, impure energy through your slightly open mouth. Close your mouth, breathing the yellow earth energy into your spleen. Open your mouth slightly and breathe out any impure energy. Repeat these steps for a few more breaths, then allow your breathing to return to normal.

From earth comes white metal, associated with lungs. When you are ready, breathe the white energy of metal, of white gold, of silver, and of pewter into your lungs through your nose. Exhale any used-up, impure energy through your slightly open mouth. Close your mouth, breathing the white metal energy into your lungs. Open your mouth slightly and breathe out any impure

Schroedinger's Lump

I found a lump,
I know it well;
I found a lump,
What tales it could tell,
If only I would let
The surgeon cut,
If only I would let
Her open me, but
Then we would know it
For foe or friend,
Then we would know it
And, starting a trend,
We'd be in one place
And not the other;
We'd be in one place
Possibilities we'd smother.
Mystery's the thing
That I do prefer;
Mystery's the thing—
Certainty would deter
From knowing the lump
And all it contains,
From knowing the lump
And the life it sustains.
I found a lump,
I know it quite well;
I found a lump,
And what tales it does tell.

This poem poured out of me a few weeks after I discovered the lump in my breast. It became my healing mantra; I recited it several times a day, especially when I felt fearful, and I still read it on occasion. I've called it "Schroedinger's Lump" in honor of the physicist who posed the following conundrum in response to recent discoveries in quantum physics: There is a cat in a box. Is it alive or dead? It is both, until you open the box, thereby collapsing the waveform of possibilities and forcing the selection of only one. Now the cat is either dead or alive, but no longer both.

energy. Repeat these steps for a few more breaths, then allow your breathing to return to normal.

From compression of metal comes blue water, associated with the kidneys. When you are ready, breathe the blue energy of water, of lakes, of rivers, of oceans into your kidneys through your nose. Exhale any used-up, impure energy out through your slightly open mouth. Close your mouth, breathing the blue water energy into your kidneys. Open your mouth slightly and breathe out any impure energy. Repeat these steps for a few more breaths, then allow your breathing to return to normal.

Stay with this breathing for a few minutes, noticing any changes in your body, your consciousness, or your breath. Slowly bring your awareness back to the world.

■ Exercise 5.2: Poetry Writing

In addition to journaling, poetry writing can enhance your transformative healing process.[3] This exercise is not about writing Pulitzer Prize–winning poems; it is about expressing your personal experience in a less linear fashion. By juxtaposing two apparently unrelated images (see the poem, "Finding Hope" below for an example). Poetry writing often opens us to new perceptions. It certainly brings us back to our creativity, which once again connects us with life.

Sit in a quiet, meditative state with paper and a pen at the ready. Allow images of your illness and healing journey to arise in your mind, and record them on paper. Note any feelings, other images, or symbols that come up. Play with putting two seemingly opposite ideas or images together from the list you just created. After a few minutes continue shaping the images and feelings into a poem. Thank your creative self when you are done.

Finding Hope

Hope is the stone
in the fist of despair —
each finger of abject fear
for which there is no solace
worries it, denies it,
will not release it.
The other hand grips
a branch
high in a tree
and the wind has
picked up.
There is a strong branch
below me, or there is not.
In times like these,
losing hope
is the only hope I have
of going down slowly.

—JERE, HUSBAND OF TAMARA

■ Exercise 5.3: Fear and Love Alchemy

Many writers, philosophers, and theologians consider love and fear to be the antithesis of each other—two sides of the same coin. I have talked about transforming fear rather than eliminating it, because it does have energy that is valuable to us. With this exercise, you have the opportunity to find your own unique way of blending the two energies into one.

Imagine that you have two balls, one representing fear and the other love. Place one in each hand and toss them back and forth, faster and faster. Notice what happens. There is no right or wrong result to this exercise; it is just a way to experience something. It can be done over and over, noticing how the result changes over time.

■ Exercise 5.4: Guided Visualization: Into the Woods[4]

If you have not read the story of Iron John (page 36), do so now. This visualization puts you into a portion of that story. As in many fairy tales, the story of Iron John uses the woods to signify the mysterious center of the self, a shadowy, scary place that is also full of great riches. This allows you to go into your own woods on a journey of discovery. Remember: if the journey becomes too scary you can always follow your breath up and out into the light of day. Also remember to bring the scary parts back with you so you can expose them to the light; you can do this by writing about them in your journal or sharing your experience with a friend. This action will reduce the ability of the scary parts to produce fear in you.

Refer to Appendix C for general instructions for grounding or visualization exercises.

Begin by connecting with your breath; take about two minutes to do this.

Remember the story of Iron John. Imagine yourself as a monarch whose kingdom includes a forest that you have forbidden anyone, including yourself, to enter. Find yourself standing at the edge of the woods, looking in but afraid to enter because of what it might hold. Take about a minute to allow yourself to experience this fully.

Now imagine yourself as the fearless hunter who asks for and receives permission from the monarch to enter the forest. Send your dog in ahead of you and then follow, remaining alert to what you are seeing, hearing, feeling, and experiencing. See what you find in your woods; take about three minutes to do this.

Now imagine yourself as Iron John or Iron Jane—the wild man or wild woman of the woods. How did you first come to be in the woods? What magic spell brought you and bound you here? How do you feel about "intruders," such as hunters or adventure seekers? What do you have hidden at the bottom of the pond? Take about three minutes with this.

Now imagine yourself as the child of the monarch. You are both intrigued by and scared of the wild person who has been brought to your castle. What questions do you have for this person? Take about two minutes with this.

Imagine that the wild person has carried you off into the woods. How do you experience this person now? How do you feel? What do you learn? Take about three minutes with this.

Now imagine you have to leave the shelter of the woods and the protection of your friend and make your way in the world. How does this feel? What encounters do you have? Take about two minutes with this.

> Some dreams try
> to loosen the hold of
> old fears and beliefs
> to set us loose.
>
> —BRENDA MURPHEE

Imagine that as you make your way in the world, you can always call to your ally in the woods for help. Imagine doing this now; call to Iron John or Jane and ask for some assistance with an issue in your life. What does your ally offer you? Take about three minutes with this.

Finally, imagine that Iron John or Jane comes to you, transformed into his or her true monarch self. Welcome and embrace your friend. How does this feel? Hold a feast in your own honor. Who is there? What are you celebrating, and how? What are all the gifts you receive? Take about four minutes with this.

Begin to move back from the inner world to the outer world by following your breath up and out, up and out, up and out. Take about two minutes with this. Gently shaking your hands and feet can help reorient you in the outer world.

■ Exercise 5.5: Dream Work

Dream work is as old as humankind. In ancient Greece entire temples were built just for people to use for dreaming. The Greeks believed dreams would give them the answers to life's problems, especially for illnesses and possible remedies. Today dreams are a largely untapped source of information, yet their wisdom remains available. Ask for a dream about your fear and

Dream Tips

1. A little rosemary placed under your pillow helps you remember your dreams.

2. Wake up slowly and gently—without an alarm—to better remember.

3. Dreams are multilayered. They may be about what you did yesterday, but they are always about much more.

4. Find at least one "dream buddy" with whom you can share your dreams, without an analysis at first. Simply sharing dreams often opens up their mysteries.[5]

5. Keep a tape recorder or a pad of paper and a pencil by your bed to record your dreams; even a single word or phrase can provide you with important information (see number 14) or help you remember more of the dream after you awake.

6. Ask your dreams to answer questions about particular issues, such as an illness or a physical symptom. Assume that any dream you have after asking such a question is an answer to that request.

7. Scary dreams are usually trying to get our attention. Ask yourself what needs attention in your life.

8. Stimulants, including chocolate, consumed around bedtime will make it difficult to fall asleep. Warm milk and chamomile tea help promote relaxation and sleep.

9. Try acting out your dreams: if you are dancing in your dreams, dance; if you are swimming in your dreams, go swimming.

10. Ask to meet your spirit guides[6] in your dreams, and see who or what shows up. These guides can be used consciously as allies in the future.

11. Rather than buying a dream dictionary create your own. Figure out what snakes, cigars, or any other symbol means to *you* by free-associating about them each time they appear in one of your dreams. Over time you will discover what meaning the symbols hold for you.

12. Collect images from magazines and create collages of your dreams. Put the collages up on a wall and let your gaze turn to them daily. In this way you will slowly discover their meaning.

13. Consciously go back into a dream and take it beyond the point where it ended. (See Exercise 5.4 for an example of imagining elaborations of a dream.)

14. A single image quite often captures a whole dream. If you feel overwhelmed by the length of a dream, select the one image or scene that carries the most energy for you. Assume that this image will take you where you want to go.

15. Dream energies often carry over into our waking lives. Use the emotion, feeling, physical sensation, or symptom with which you awake as you would a dream. Lie still, taking some time with the sensation; breathe into it, and allow some images to form in response. Share the whole experience with your dream buddy and see what other insights or awarenesses this raises.

how to move through it, and trust that any dream you have answers this question. Then work with the dream.[7] (See the side-bar Dream Tips on pages 97–98. In addition Exercise 5.4, a guided visualization for exploring the story of Iron John demon-strates a process you can apply to dream work.)

■ Exercise 5.6: Radiating Love

Research suggests that the heart not only influences the body's internal well-being, but also acts as a radio transmitter "broad-casting" into the environment. This substantiates the old saying that no person is an island. By radiating our inner experience of love outward, we create changes in the world around us.

Whenever you feel full of love, be sure you send some of it out to other people who could use it. You can send it to friends, fam-ily members, members of your church, or even strange enemies, and people thousands of miles away. (See the sidebar on page 100 for an example.) Ram Dass, a former psychologist and well-known speaker and teacher of yoga, meditation, and a variety of spiritual practices, including Hinduism, karma, and Sufism, talks fre-quently about this practice.

■ Exercise 5.7: Embracing Fear

In Exercise 2.3 you honored your fear, acknowledging its role in trying to keep you safe from harm. Now it's time to actually embrace the fear and make friends with it. During this journey we have learned that the fear and the energy it creates is actually yours. Banishing fear doesn't really solve anything; that is the main lesson of Iron John. But by embracing fear you keep that energy for yourself, making it work for you instead of against you.

Imagine the fear is standing in front of you. Acknowledge it and then put your arms around it. Take the visualization further, imag-ining the fear melting and flowing into you through your pores, fill-ing your body with its transformed energy. See yourself as whole.

Radiating Love

Donna, a woman I met in a one of my workshops, tells a remarkable story about the power of radiating love:

"I saw a woman walking out of the mall with her little boy, and screaming at him with so much hatred in her voice, calling him every name and saying things like, 'You're stupid.' The little boy was crying and holding her hand. All I wanted to do was pick him up and hold him, but I knew I couldn't. I had to do something, so I started in the woman's direction, wondering what I was going to do. Without really thinking about it, I went to this place of love, even for her. When I walked over to where she was, I looked straight at her, without any fear and not caring what would happen to me because I knew I was okay, and I said, 'Would you like me to get you some help? Do you need me to get you some help?' She changed instantly, smiling and saying, 'No, that's okay, I'm fine now.'"

■ Exercise 5.8: Tonglen

Tonglen, which translates as "giving and receiving," is a Buddhist practice that can take many shapes. For our purposes, it is a meditation in which you "give all profit and gain to others, take all loss and defeat on yourself."[8] That is, you absorb the pain and suffering of others (including yourself), and then breathe love and compassion into the situation. When the meditation is done correctly, the love and compassion you experience internally are not compromised or lessened, but are actually increased because they are infinite. This is an advanced exercise that should be attempted only after considerable other work is done.

Take as long as you need to ground and center yourself through breath. You can also use one of the grounding tools in Exercises 4.5A, B, C, and D. When you are ready, think of a situation in your life that is causing you fear or some other kind of distress. Breathe that distress into your body—which, by virtue of being grounded and centered, can easily cope with the distress by purifying it or allowing it to flow down into the earth, where it is dispersed. Now breathe into that situation love and compassion, or any other feeling that seems appropriate. Do this for several breaths. If you begin to feel overwhelmed, stop immediately and begin again only after recentering and grounding. This can be done for another by breathing in what you perceive as their distress, and breathing out love and compassion. This can be used to diffuse a tense situation or offer help to someone who is not present.

> *When I focused on my heart and transcended my brain's fears about its body, I could feel the energy of those I loved enveloping, soothing, and healing me.*
>
> —PAUL PEARSALL,
> THE HEART'S CODE:
> TAPPING THE WISDOM AND
> POWER OF OUR HEART ENERGY

WORK WITH PARTNERS OR ALLIES

■ Exercise 5.9: Dialoguing from the Third Chakra (Power)

Practice talking, or dialoguing, with a friend from your third chakra. This is the power chakra, which governs self-empowerment and shared power with (not over) others. This exercise is about speaking from your truth and your strength; it is not a time for humility, but honesty. Remember to breathe into your belly as you practice. This dialogue should include giving each other feedback. Whenever you catch your friend speaking from a place other than truth or strength, speak up. Your friend should do the same for you.

During one of her radio shows, Dr. Laura Schlessinger described a friend as "one who is willing to risk the friendship by telling you the truth when you are about to hurt yourself." We need to be such a friend to ourselves as well. Not being honest about who you are and what your strengths are hurts you—and everyone else, for you are then withholding some of the gifts you have to offer others.

■ Exercise 5.10: Dialoguing from the Fourth Chakra (Love)

Practice talking, or dialoguing, with a friend from your fourth, or love, chakra. This exercise involves speaking about and from your love, compassion, and caring; it reveals another kind of truth about who you are. The exercise gives you an opportunity to look beneath your anger, hate, and prejudice and find the truth of your love. Remember to breathe into your heart as you practice. This dialogue should include giving each other feedback. Whenever you catch your friend speaking from a place other than truth or love, speak up. Your friend should do the same for you.

Family and Friends Should Be Responsible for Their Own Fears

Polly was a massage therapist, acupuncturist, and herbology student. Within twelve months, she watched both of her parents die. Although each experience was unique, she was able to bring some of her healing arts to both situations.

Polly made a very physical connection with her mother through massage and acupuncture. And she provided her father, who was dying of kidney failure, with some herbs for easing discomfort. At the same time as she was making these positive connections, her fears of losing her parents and of being overwhelmed by their deaths also caused her to connect with them in unhealthy fear-based ways. Eventually she was able to recognize this, let go, and be more present.

While Polly's father was in the hospital she was confronted by his physician, who wanted to know about the herbs she was giving her father. Though this was not an unreasonable request, he was implying that Polly's actions were the reason her father was dying. This frightened her. Polly immediately checked with one of her instructors, an ally, who assured her that the herbs were not contributing to her father's deterioration. But out of anger at what she perceived as the doctor's insensitivity and her fear of the doctor's power, Polly withheld the information, rationalizing that it would mean nothing to him anyway. She later realized that the information might have enhanced the doctor's ability to make her father more comfortable, which is what she had been trying to do with the herbs.

A year later Polly's mother had a recurrence of cancer. The cancer was inoperable, and even with two different chemotherapies there was only a 5 percent chance of improvement. Polly's mother decided to forgo treatment and stay at home. Polly recalls, "My instinct, being the outsider . . . was, 'You've got to try whatever, don't you? You can't just say no.'" But her mother never changed her mind. Polly, the healer, kept looking for new ways to help, while her mother tried a few alternative therapies. "I felt like I needed to control the situation a little bit," Polly says, "and finally, after a few days, I realized I had no control and I had to accept it in every fiber." Polly felt a shift in herself, and she was able to be a little more relaxed. This change in perception allowed her to be receptive to her mother. "[I was able to] just stay open, feel everything I felt, be willing to experience everything, be there, be aware, and not to waste a moment."

Exercises for Disconnecting from Others' Fears

While we may be taking responsibility for our own fears, no longer radiating them out into the environment where they can affect others, some people may still be burdening us with their fears. The following exercises are designed to help us disconnect from those fears.

■ Exercise 5.11A: Disconnecting by Cutting the Cords

Chakra theory includes *cording*, the concept of connecting energetically with others at the sites of our chakras. It is as though we send a cord out from one of our chakras—where we feel especially vulnerable or unsure of ourselves—and attach to someone else's chakra in order to draw strength from them or give them energy.

When we get sick we are especially vulnerable. Our illness affects everyone around us, stirring some into action and others into reaction. Many people experience the illness as happening or capable of happening to them; it rouses some of their worst fears, which they may transmit to you via cording. When we are ill and afraid, we have enough to deal with without having to take care of those around us. Feel free to detach from these people's fears in any way you can in order to take care of yourself.

In your mind's eye, scan your body and look for any "cords" going out from or attaching to you. Gently withdraw the cords from the other person if you have sent them out or disengage the cords from yourself if someone else sent them your way. If these cords come back you may need to be more assertive or even aggressive, cutting the cords with an imaginary knife and then cauterizing the ends with an imaginary flame.

Obviously, this exercise is important for friends, family, and care-givers who might be cording with you. (See the sidebar Family and Friends Should Be Responsible for Their Own Fears on pages 102–103 for an example.)

■ Exercise 5.11B: Disconnecting Through Affirmations

Over the years, affirmations have gotten a bad rap. While I would agree that sweet, generalized sentimentalities uttered in a distracted manner are probably not all that useful, I am a firm believer in the value of precisely worded phrases that are repeated with strong intention. After all, we have probably become fear-based in part by repeating and assimilating negative thoughts about ourselves over and over for many years. With affirmations we have the opportunity to replace those unconscious negative thoughts with concepts that are truthful and more beneficial.

> I had a brain cancer specialist sit in my living room and tell me that he would never take radiation if he had a brain tumor. And I asked him, "But, do you send people for radiation?" and he said, "Of course; I'd be drummed out of the hospital if I didn't."
>
> —RALPH MOSS, PH.D., IN AN INTERVIEW IN THE JANUARY 1998 *TOWNSEND LETTER FOR DOCTORS AND PATIENTS*

Here is an affirmation that I have found powerful in disconnecting from others' fears: It is my consciousness, not the consciousness of others, that shapes and molds my world. This is just one example of; if it doesn't resonate well with you, create one (or more) that does. Here are some other possibilities:

When I feel attacked (emotionally, mentally or spiritually) by someone, I will imagine it as a "call for love," and base my response on that; conversely, when I attack another, I will look for the fear behind it, and ask for love and compassion for myself;

The more I am my true, powerful self, the more I have everything I really want, including my health;

I forgive myself for holding back or holding out;

I empower myself and others;

I give my fears over to God and live from my true nature instead.

Susan's Story:
Standing Up for Yourself in the Healing Process

Susan had just completed a college degree late in life, after her children had grown and left home, and she was just beginning to enjoy her new career when she was diagnosed with ovarian cancer. Because this kind of cancer is so powerful and there is no "standard" treatment that is regularly successful, Susan was put on an experimental treatment protocol. The problem with such protocols is that once you begin it the doctors want you to stay in it, regardless of your experience, because that is how they learn what works and what doesn't.

According to her husband, Doug, Susan was quite a trooper; she went along with the protocol, even when it became apparent that the level of toxicity from the treatment was quite high and was making her more sick than the cancer itself. Susan and Doug had never been told up front that they would probably be buying a few more months of time, but at the price of incredible discomfort. In fact, says Doug, "the medications themselves became life-threatening—from a night at the opera to the emergency room in five hours." After that, both Susan and Doug had a lot of fear in relation to the drugs.

Susan wanted very much to attend her daughter's graduation from college, but she didn't want to put herself at risk in the middle of a farm community (the drugs suppressed her immune system), where the college was located. She decided to discontinue the treatment protocol. The nurses supported Susan, but the doctors really wanted her to stay on the treatment. But Doug comments, "Susan was strong enough to overcome that." Although she was sick without the drugs, the next course of drug treatment was life-threatening.

Once, Susan wanted to leave the hospital for a few hours for a colleague's wedding, so the nurses helped her get ready. Again, the doctors didn't want her to go. "These are non-healing tensions," Doug relates, "and there is fear, because you know you're on the edge a little bit." For Doug and Susan, attending support groups was a way to transform the fear, so that they could "learn to live in the moment, to make the most out of the days they had left." He concludes, "That was healing."

■ Exercise 5.11C: Disconnecting from the Fears of Our Health Care Providers

We must find health care providers who are aware of their own fears, just as we are aware of ours. If they are conscious of and work on their fears, they will be less of a chance likely to transmit their fears onto us. If they work out of their fears, it means that they are less able to see you as an individual and probably will want you to make the healing choices they would choose for themselves—or the healing choices their profession typically dictates. The stronger they feel about this and the more pressure they experience from their colleagues, the more likely they are to use fear in an effort to convince you of the correctness of their recommendations.

Because this is an especially vulnerable time for you, you should never agree to any invasive treatment the first time you are confronted with it; take time to think about it. Take a prepared ally in to the doctor's office when you are discussing treatment options. Do not be afraid of offending fear-instilling practitioners by terminating your relationship with them if their "help" becomes more of a burden. And feel free to modify certain treatment recommendations you do accept in order to make them really work for you. (By this, I am not recommending that you do anything obviously dangerous for yourself, such as taking more than the suggested dose of a prescribed drug, which could have serious, toxic effects. For an example of healthy modifications, see the sidebar Susan's Story on pages 106–107.)

■ Exercise 5.12: Guided Visualization: All the World's a Stage

This exercise allows you to create your own theater, stage, and life "play"; practice difficult conversations or situations in advance; and disconnect from anyone whose energy is not loving or healing.

Refer to Appendix C for general instructions for grounding and visualization exercises.

Begin by connecting with your breath; remember to take the breath deep into your belly, your place of wisdom and power. Take about two minutes to do this.

As you continue to breathe into your belly, notice what your belly center looks and feels like, including such characteristics as color, temperature, structure, tone, or quality. Stay with this for about three to five minutes, until you feel truly grounded in your sense of self.

From the belly center, allow yourself to imagine that you are up on a stage in a theater that is totally yours. The play being enacted is your life. Look around and become familiar with the theater, the stage, and how you feel about being here. Is this a one-person show? Do you want it to be? Remember, this is your theater, your stage, your life, and you get to choose how you want it to proceed. You can even change it at a moment's notice. If you're not alone on stage but want to be, choose a way to make the other players leave. If you are alone but don't want to be, invite some other people to play with you. Remember, however, that once you choose to allow other people on stage, you may not have complete control over how they play their parts; on the other hand, they may be willing to take some direction and play out different scenarios with you. Since you are the author and director, you can ask certain players to leave the stage if you don't like what is happening. If they don't leave, you can always end the play by closing the curtain, turning off the lights, and leaving the theater. You can try again at another time.

Now check out the audience. Who is in it? Are they cheering you on? Judging you? Heckling? You get to decide if they stay or not; you make up the rules for how the audience members are to behave if they are going to remain in your theater. If you don't want someone there, simply imagine an usher escorting that person to an exit. (You don't even have to give them a refund!)

You can use the audience in many ways. Imagine it filled with all of your biggest supporters or allies—alive or dead, real or fictional. If there is anyone with whom you are struggling—a spouse, parent, friend, physician—try putting that person in the middle of a supportive audience and direct a monologue at him or her, saying everything you have been afraid to say because it didn't feel safe. At the end of the play, feel free to step back, close the curtain, dim the lights, and walk away.

Remember: this is your theater, your audience, your stage, your play, and your cast of characters. Do whatever you need to do to complete this image in a way that makes you feel safe and secure in your life.

When you are ready, follow your breath back up and out into the world.

Work with Groups: Healing Circles

Research suggests that the power of a group is exponentially superior to the power of an individual in its ability to facilitate the healing process.[9] Thus, while asking for individual friends' support in your work with fear is helpful, gathering them all together in one place at one time for a specific purpose is that much better. While healing circles can be quite elaborabe in their design, they do not need to be. Recently I suffered from a very high fever as a secondary complication of both Lyme disease and a staph infection. A friend was so worried about me that she spent the night at my house to make sure I drank enough fluids. She also called a few friends and asked them to meditate on my getting well at ten that night and seven the next morning. On both occasions, shortly after the time she specified, my temperature plummeted from 104 to below 98.6 degrees. This demonstrates how the healing circle can be simple and nonlocal—the healers do not have to be together in the same physical location or with the person being healed.

Walton's Qigong Healing Circle

This exercise was created for a friend, Walton, who was physically absent from the circle because of an illness that caused him to be hospitalized. Although this is an example of distance or nonlocal healing,[10] it can be applied to a person who is sitting in the middle of the circle.

This is the sequence we followed in the healing circle:

1. Think of your love for our friend. Speak it out loud.

2. Bring in his energy body; imagine him sitting in the middle of the circle. Call on any healers you know, such as Jesus, Buddha, or your ancestors.

3. Cleanse his energy body of any illness you see or feel, using one hand to pull out impurities or wipe the auric field clean. Place any impurities you gather in your other hand, as if you were filling a balloon.

4. Holding the impure energy in one hand, clap with the other, saying "gone" each time you clap. Speed

up the clapping and image the energy being dispersed to the far ends of the universe.

5. See our friend bathed in the white light of your heart's love. Do this for ten to fifteen minutes.

6. Let him go back to his physical body.

7. Rub your hands together; massage your face.

8. Thank and release any healing presences you called forth.

Walton's wife comments, "He used a lot of Qigong when he was in the hospital. I know it worked; he would always have some kind of dramatic change after that or the prayer circles. It happened three times. I would leave, and he'd be in really bad shape, and I'd come in the next day after a prayer circle, and he would have had a radical change for the better."

■ Exercise 5.13A: The Laughing Circle

This is a group version of Exercise 4.14: The Inner Smile. You'll need a group of at least five people. Each person should lie down, creating a closed circle of interwoven bodies, with the head of each person resting on the belly of another. One person begins by saying "ha." The next person says "ha-ha," with each person building the "chain" of laughter until the whole group is laughing spontaneously. This exercise can be used to begin or close any group gathering as a way of bringing all the participants out of fear and into their heart spaces.

■ Exercise 5.13B: A Qigong Healing Circle

Although there are many types of healing circles, the one I am most familiar with is a Qigong healing circle which some of my friends learned from a local Qigong mater. It was typically led by people very familiar with energy work, and their ability to combine and focus all our energies added to the incredible healing that took place. For an outline of this particular circle (there are many styles of Qigong), please see the sidebar Walton's Qigong Healing Circle pages 110–111.

The healing circle I describe in Exercise 5.14 is rather elaborate, but simple circles can work just as well.

> *True prayer and love are really learned in the hour when prayer becomes impossible and your heart turns to stone.*
>
> —THOMAS MERTON,
> NEW SEEDS OF CONTEMPLATION

■ Exercise 5.14: Ritual and Ceremony

Part of the healing circle's power is in gathering energy for a specific purpose in a format that has been used repeatedly, thus creating a positive morphic field. (Refer to the introduction for an explanation of morphic fields.) The more elements of ritual or ceremony that are added to these gatherings, the more powerful the meetings seem to become. Whether the gatherings are explicitly religious or secular in nature seems not to matter as much as the focus of energy and the intent.

Most rituals entail the use of the following elements (note that all of these were present in Walton's Qigong Healing Circle):

- The creation of a sacred or special space within which the ceremony takes place; this is used both for protection and containment—so that the energy being created does not leak out. This is often done with candles, incense, and the "creation" of a circle by drawing its outline with chalk, salt, or some other means; rooms, churchs, and labyrinths also serve this purpose.

- Asking for being witnessed by or supported by various allies, such as religious figures, angels, ancestors, spirit guides, earth elements, mentors, etc.

Heal, Baby, Heal

Jan is a longtime nurse. About ten years ago she was in a car accident that broke her right femur in several places. Her first surgery did not go well, and she was in incredible pain for about ten months. Then the plate that held together her leg bone broke. She was taken to the emergency room, where a doctor she had never met before decided that immediate surgery was necessary. Jan recalls, "I said to him, 'I have to ask you to do something for me. In the operating room, you must not say anything negative, like *Oops, This is a mess,* or *This will never heal,* because I believe I will hear it.' Well, he looked at me like I had just climbed out of an alien spaceship.

After the surgery I wake up, and for the first time in a year I'm able to lift both my legs off the bed and up to the ceiling, pain-free. I'm ecstatic. The surgeon walks in and he tells me about the surgery and what he found, and tells me that during the surgery they kept saying, 'Heal, baby, heal.' Isn't that just too wonderful? That had to be so foreign to who he was, but he did it!"

This is a great example of an affirmation as a prayer. It also demonstrates how important it is to stand up for yourself, and how simple the request you make can be.

- The (re)enactment of some intention, myth, or belief. This may look like a performance, and often involves some kind of movement, such as dance.

- The expression of gratitude for the experience and eventual (positive) outcome.

- The closing of the circle and return to daily life.

■ Exercise 5.15: The Special Case of Prayer

Religious leaders and spiritually minded individuals have known all along about the power of prayer. Finally, Western medicine is catching up.[11] Some of the power of prayer appears to lie in our acknowledging our inability to control the situation, surrendering our picture of the outcome, and asking for help from a power greater than ourselves. For example, many years ago I suffered from an internal parasite. I had been given a liquid antidote, the most vile syrup I had ever tasted. Somehow I got through a whole bottle of this stuff, having been told that one bottle would be enough to kill the parasite. When I went back to the healer who was helping me, she told me the parasite was not yet gone and I would have to use another bottle of the syrup. I bought the bottle, took a swig from it, and threw it up, unable to swallow even one more dose. In tears, I prayed for assistance. I received this answer: "The parasite is gone; all you had to do was ask." The next day I saw the healer briefly, who confirmed that the parasite was gone, having been "burned to ash."

So prayer works "miracles," but what is prayer? Was it prayer when my friends meditated for me? Was it prayer when Jan's doctor said, "Heal, baby, heal?" (See the sidebar Heal, Baby, Heal on page 113.) The truth is that we don't really know what prayer is, and it seems to be different for every individual.[12] Sometimes it even seems to be different depending on the context.[13] Sometimes prayer is silent, sometimes it is spoken aloud. Sometimes it is words, sometimes images. Gregg Braden describes a Native American man who "prayed rain"; he didn't ask

---

Church Going Boosts Immune System

—HEADLINE IN THE JANUARY 1998 *TOWNSEND LETTER FOR DOCTORS AND PATIENTS*

■

HMO Officials: Spirituality Can Aid Healing

—HEADLINE IN THE DECEMBER 22, 1997 *LOS ANGELES TIMES*

■

I don't know how to forgive, but I can pray for him.

—ANONYMOUS PERSON AT A WISDOM WAYS GATHERING AT ST. CATHERINE'S UNIVERSITY IN ST. PAUL, MINNESOTA

for rain to be sent but instead visualized it already happening, and then felt gratitude.[14] Perhaps prayer is all these things and more—something our "logical" minds will never be able to pin down or make sense of.

SUMMARY

By now you are well on your way to being a responder, rather than a reactor, to fear. If you are in any way involved in the health care profession, I encourage you to explore the comments and exercises in chapter 6. If you're not, there is still one area for you to explore: the fear of death. We have touched on this a couple times, but we will go into more depth in chapter 7. I believe that the fear of death underlies all other fears, and unless we deal with it we will continue to be unconscious of our fears—and they will continue to haunt us.

6
Exercises for
Health Care Professionals

In all kinds of Tibetan medicine, the interactive role of the healer is emphasized. "Affectionate care" is considered to be an important factor in the recovery of the patient. The moral quality of the healer, his or her depth of wisdom and compassion, is believed to be directly related to the ability to effect a cure.

—TERRY GIFFORD, *TIBETAN BUDDHIST MEDICINE AND PSYCHIATRY: THE DIAMOND HEALING*

To the extent that we practitioners carry our own fears into the consulting room, we add to patients' fears, making it more difficult for them to find their own paths of healing. While offering this workbook to your patients, clients, colleagues, or employees who are experiencing fear will be helpful, transforming your own fears will ultimately be of more value. In this chapter I talk about how providers can use the previous exercises, and I add a few exercises that are specific to health care professionals. I focus on primary care-givers—particularly medical doctors—but I invite anyone who works directly with patients to use any of the exercises that seem appropriate.

116

It May Not Be What You Think It Is

Leslie, the doula and business coach we met earlier, once worked with a physician whose client, having developed a fairly debilitating disease, asked him to sign a work-release order. The doctor was reluctant to do this because he found no neurological problem that would keep her from working. The woman understood this, but insisted that she couldn't work because it was simply too stressful and tiring for her. When the doctor refused to sign the order the woman said, "Well, you just don't know what it's like to have this disease." Enraged, the doctor said, "I hate it when people say that to me; that just makes me crazy."

As Leslie helped the doctor process what had happened, he realized that when people told him, "You don't understand," he heard, "You are incompetent." Leslie explains, "I think for a lot of doctors there is a fear of not being seen as competent; that's what their whole school experience is about—never not having the answers, never saying, 'I don't know,' always being on top of their game. And when a patient is talking about feelings, they equate that with knowledge. So, I think that's a fear that doctors have—they fear that people are going to think they're stupid."

For most health care providers, it is important to realize that, very often, fear lies beneath other feelings such as anger, resentment, and even bravado. While there is a lot to be afraid of in the health care system, our being afraid and not acknowledging it actually augments to the fear, which impedes our ability to assist the people who come to us for help. It may also inhibit their own healing capacities.

■ **Exercise 6.1: Recognizing Fear**

The need for my diagnoses to be free of error can provoke unwanted stress.

—SPENCE NADLER, "A WOMAN WITH BREAST CANCER," *HARPER'S* MAGAZINE, JUNE 1997

In my experience—and that of some of my colleagues—health care providers (medical doctors, in particular) have difficulty recognizing that they are afraid. This is instilled, at least in part, by the medical educational system, which makes it a taboo to be afraid, let alone talk about it with anyone.

The first step is to review the exercises in chapter 1 and begin to identify the faces of your fear. Here is a list of possibilities to get you started:

- fear of being wrong
- fear of harming someone
- fear of being sued for malpractice
- fear of being dropped by your professional liability insurance company or of having your rates raised
- fear of losing control of your practice to an HMO
- fear of being overlooked for a promotion
- fear of being found out for the impostor you imagine yourself to be
- fear of losing your income
- fear of being fired
- fear of being seen as incompetent by patients or other professionals
- fear of being found incompetent by your licensing board

Also see the sidebar Why I Quit: A Doctor Speaks Out, pages 119–120.

Why I Quit: A Doctor Speaks Out

Lorraine was a plastic surgeon with a very valuable specialty. "I was doing extremely well with my practice," she says, "and it surprised the community when I left medicine." Although several unrelated factors suddenly coalesced to trigger her decision to quit, fear was "a huge factor." She remarks, "I knew that I did not know everything, nor could I, and therefore I was very fearful of being in a situation where I might not choose the best treatment option, either from lack of knowledge or lack of experience. I feared having a complication, whether it be my fault or not, and being criticized by my peers or the community. I feared being responsible for a poor result on a patient. I even feared killing a patient. I also feared not being able to live up to the reputation that I had developed or the trust that my patients had in me. I had fear from knowing that I did not know everything and that I would have to use my patients as "guinea pigs" if I were to try a new technique or a surgery I had not done before. I have never had a lawsuit against me, and will fear it until the seven-year statute of limitations is up."

Lorraine continues, "I was not aware of fear affecting the recovery of my patients. Certainly there was lots of fear in the patients themselves. However, I can say that it was very often apparent that a positive attitude definitely affected a patient's outcome . . . in life-threatening situations." She tried to present all the details and give her patients positive thoughts to help minimize their fears. But Lorraine's fear affected her practice, as she became compulsive with her treatments. "I followed my patients very closely. I did any part of the treatment that was important myself. I would see my patients frequently until I was sure that all would go well on its own."

Looking back on her practice, Lorraine notes, "It is basically taboo to discuss your fears with anyone. I would discuss them only with good friends who also went into medicine and who were not in my community. No one ever admits that they have fear or that they don't know everything."

I am saddened by Lorraine's withdrawal from medicine, as I believe she is exactly the kind of doctor we need. I can't help but think that if she had been able to talk about her concerns more openly, perhaps even as far back as in medical school, and if she could have gotten feedback like Leslie's (see the sidebar Information, Please on pages 60–63), she might have felt the support necessary to continue her valuable work.

■ **Exercise 6.2: Reporting Fear**

In Exercises 2.2A-C we explored the benefits of saying your fears aloud. Though it may feel incredibly risky, the best possible place to do this is with a group of colleagues. Why? So that you can know you are not alone. It is one thing for a friend or spouse to empathize, but quite another for a colleague, who is in the same boat as you are, to say that he or she feels the same vulnerabilities, frailties, and uncertainties as you.

I once gathered with a group of about forty of my colleagues. Everyone was asked to write their fears on slips of paper, which were then placed in a bowl. We passed the bowl around, and each person drew a slip of paper and took turns reading the fears aloud. The relief that came from hearing my own fears repeated over and over by others was incredible. We then used those pieces of paper to fire a clay pot upon which we had inscribed our dreams for ourselves and our profession. The pot was then circulated through the community so that everyone could remember that evening's ritual.

If you really feel you can't trust a colleague with this information (another fear?), then seek out your husband, wife, sister, brother, best friend, or even a counselor with whom you can share this information. If it's eating you alive, it's affecting your work and your patients. Saying it aloud starts moving the fear outside of you.

I didn't really care if I lived or died. . . . But when I walked into [his] office, I felt a sense of peace. He didn't rush, and he was an excellent listener. I trusted him.

—JOANNE BROOKER, "DOCTORS WHO PRAY WITH THEIR PATIENTS," *GOOD HOUSEKEEPING*, JANUARY 1998

■ Exercise 6.3: Releasing Fear

Any of the exercises in chapter 3 will help you, but I have found Exercises 3.4 and 3.6A, B, and C to be especially beneficial. Many of us went into the healing professions because we had idealistic desires to help people, to help the world. Often it was tough slogging through the tedium of our degree programs just to get to the point where we could do the work we felt called to do. Finally we get to a hospital or clinic, only to discover that there is even more tedium, more red tape, lots of paperwork, lots of "turf" issues, and now, with HMOs and DRGs, limitations on what is considered to be therapeutic or appropriate. Thus, opportunities for true healing work seem minimal. When our bubble is burst we often feel grief, depression, and anger—which may just be other faces of fear.

The key to healing is tapping into a person's belief system, and working with the individual to maximize the healing experience and potential.

—LINDA, FORMER MEDICAL STUDENT

■ Exercise 6.4: Replacing Fear

Chapters 4 and 5 are loaded with excellent exercise for replacing fear that apply fully to health care providers. In particular, Exercise 4.10 helps you create a talisman which you can take with you into meetings with insurance adjusters, consultations with patients, or any other place where you are likely to encounter fear. Exercise 4.12 teaches you to breathe into your heart space as a way of keeping fears at bay; then, in Exercise 5.6, you learn to radiate that love out to others (i.e., colleagues, patients, managers) so as to help reduce the overall field of fear. It can also be helpful to learn how to disconnect from others' fears as Exercise 5.11A, B and C directs; this can help stop the flow of fear back into the soft, loving space you are (re)developing in your heart.

EXERCISES FOR LISTENING AND GATHERING INFORMATION

Exercises 4.1A and B help us to cope with the fears which come about from having too little or too much information. I remember walking into a consultation room my first week of graduate school, convinced that I didn't know enough to be helpful; it can be just as scary to have so much information that you can't see the client in front of you for all the case studies you have read.

As professionals, most of our information comes from textbooks, professors, colleagues, lab work, and drug company pamphlets citing supportive research. Sometimes we can walk into an inital interview with someone whose chart we've read thinking that we already know what will help them. This attitude is further reinforced by the current pressures to be cost effective. This leaves us not only with too little or

Will the Real Patient Please Stand Up?

Besides wanting more information from their health care providers, most people also want to be real—to be themselves—and to be seen for who they really are. This takes as many forms as there are people. For instance, I wanted to have my health care assistants listen with me to the information my dreams provided. Here is what some other people have wanted, or what helped them:

Karen, a medical doctor: "It's been my experience that if a client is intuitive she's frightening. But if you respond in fear, she'll begin to hold back important information."

Doug, on his wife Susan's experience: "I've heard that you actually shouldn't want to be such a good patient, you really have to get in their faces. But why do you have to do that? Why can't you be yourself, but have enough help in a non-medical way so you can keep it all in perspective? In this way, you don't have to adopt a persona to do battle with the faults of the system."

Sarah: "I had repeated episodes of the 'three Hs' [howling, head banging, and hyperventilating], and I was becoming suicidal." She had difficulty finding a health care resource but finally found someone who was helpful. "She picked up the phone and called the Community Mental Health Center, saying that she was referring me to them. Then she told me, 'They won't help you unless they think you're a crisis case. Don't hold back the tears.' I sat in their waiting room for three hours, every minute growing more and more afraid that I would be told, 'Sorry, we're closing now, come back tomorrow.' I began to cry and couldn't stop. The duty nurse saw this and took me next."

Betsy: "I would know I was hemorrhaging and call. They wouldn't believe or trust my knowledge of my own body. I spoke with a doctor friend who told me lots of women had heavy periods; even she didn't acknowledge that I might be hemorraging but I was. I started thinking this was normal; I lost my own value of what I know of myself. Finally I found Val, who was totally there for me. She helped me learn to listen to and trust my own body again. 'Bottom line, Betsy,' she said, 'you're the one who knows.'"

too much information, it also leaves us with an imbalance in the type of information at our disposal.

If you go back to Ken Wilber's model on page 17, almost all of the information we have at this point if from the upper right hand quadrant. It does not take into account the patient's own internal experience (see Betsy's story in the sidebar Will the Real Patient Please Stand Up? on page 123), his or her culture (see the sidebar A Hmong Patient's Story), your team members' wisdom, or even your own intuitive sense.

The following exercises offer some additional ways of gathering important information while also building trust and partnership with patients and colleagues. Building trust can be one of the quickest methods of dispelling fear.

A HMONG PATIENT'S STORY

This story came to me during of an in-service I attended on traditional Hmong spirituality. It was told by Phun Ziong, M.D., a resident in the Health East Family Practice program at Bethesda Hospital in St. Paul, Minnesota.

One Hmong patient wouldn't respond to his doctor's request to do an urgent surgical procedure. The doctor approached him twice, once on the afternoon of his admittance and again the following morning. After these two attempts, which totaled about five minutes of his time, the doctor said he was "fed up" and walked away, instructing the nursing staff to discharge the patient, as he was just taking up bed space. When Dr. Ziong approached the patient and asked why he had not given the doctor an answer, the patient said, "The doctor approached me very forcefully, and gave me only two minutes to decide. He was so harsh, so impatient—I was afraid that if I let him do it he would do it too fast and maybe do something wrong." In the Hmong culture, Ziong notes, no one makes such a momentous decision alone; they make it only when surrounded by family and friends who offer their input. "This man's family had not yet arrived, so the man could not have given the doctor an answer even if he had wanted to," she explains.

■ **Exercise 6.5A: Listening to the Patient**

It's imortant to listen deeply. It's also important to cultivate the "third ear" that Theodore Reik talks about—that is, the ability to listen to the metacommunications embedded in the patient's recitation of symptoms. But even beyond all that, I believe we should really listen to and invite the patient's inner wisdom or inner knowing. After living in his or her body for a lifetime, the patient knows more about it than you can possibly know in a few minutes or from a whole slew of tests. So take a deep breath, put your paper and pen aside, look at your patient as he or she talks, and really listen to all that is being conveyed.

■ **Exercise 6.5B: Listening to the Patient's Friends, Family, Culture, and Mythology**

Sometimes patients are incapable of talking—for example, if they're comatose or closed off because of fear, or if they don't speak the same language as you. And sometimes you simply need the additional information other sources can provide. This doesn't necessarily mean you need to go to a library and bone up on the patient's cultural history, but by listening deeply you may find the piece of information that has been eluding you. (See the sidebar A Hmong Patient's Story on page 124.) However, if you are starting to see a large number of patients from a particular cultural background, it

How did the medical profession ever develop the notion that its values should take precedence over those of patients and the public?

—LYNN PAYER, *MEDICINE AND CULTURE*

■

I began to see that the diagnosis of a disease plays little part in the healing process; nor, for that matter, does the treatment strategy. Help attuned to individual needs is what heals.

—SPENCE NADLER, "A WOMAN WITH BREAST CANCER," *HARPER'S* MAGAZINE, JUNE 1997

would be beneficial for you to get some information about their culture, especially as it relates to health care and values.

■ Exercise 6.5C: Listening to Your Team

For whatever reason—much of the time it's the fear of being seen as incompetent—many physicians act like Lone Rangers, which can get incredibly lonely and scary. The truth is that not every one of your patients is going to confide in you with those important little tidbits. Sometimes it is the dietician, or the nurse, or the occupational or physical therapist who has the best rapport with the patient. (See the sidebar Modal Hospital on page 134–36 for an illustration.) It might even help to think of the patient as the team leader. This is not a comment on you or your competence; the best dancers in the world don't always dance well with each other. So let go of that fear and let someone else on the team take the lead.

■ Exercise 6.5D: Listening to Yourself

The symptoms the patient describes and the ones you observe with your eyes, ears, and nose are all important, as is the mental sorting into diagnostic categories. But you must also listen to your intuition. I have watched a number of "psychics"—people who have honed their intuitive skills—work over the years. Most of them use some kind of "objective" tool just like your "tests"; these can take the form of an astrology chart, a deck of cards, or the palm of a person's hand. And they can point to the specific places in these "tests" where their diagnoses come from. But I have the sense that these people are tapping into something deeper that is internal; they close their eyes and look within rather than without. This is what I encourage you to do.

Medical Education as Cult

Linda, a former medical student, says of her training, "I've seen the indoctrination methods involved in Western medical training. Most physicians don't even believe there is another way of providing medical care. What scares me is what medical education does to continue this belief. It was like being brainwashed, or in a cult; there is the sleep deprivation, the food deprivation, and then the indoctrination. Self-care is not praised. The process tries to beat you into submission until, before you know it, you buy into the story."

It also might be helpful to understand that you are in a minority culture: Western medicine. This is not mainstream American culture, nor is it the culture of world medicine, which actually is quite varied. But it is a culture nonetheless, with its own language and beliefs. It resembles American culture in the sense that a large percentage of Americans when traveling abroad expect other cultures to come to them; they look for familiar American icons (like fast-food restaurants) and don't bother learning the language, simply assuming that others will speak English. That's fine if you want *The Accidental Tourist* experience—travel in a hygienic, sanitized, Americanized bubble. But this approach to healing does not work. In fact, it is the health care provider who must meet the patient more than halfway.

After you have talked with and really listened to a patient for a few minutes, close your eyes for a few moments and listen deeply to yourself. What emotions and sensations are you feeling inside? Are any images coming to you, as if in a dream? Did you have an unusual dream last night that is being called forth now, as you sit regarding this person in front of you? (Jungian therapists always take into account "first dreams," or dreams they and their clients have the night before they meet for the first time. They view the dreams as indicative of the direction the whole therapeutic process will take.) Don't try to figure out anything as you would usually do with the "objective" tests and symptom checklist; let your intuition guide you to a final question for the patient, a simple test you might not otherwise do, or a thought you wish to share with your patient. You don't need to fully understand what comes up. Sometimes in working with my clients, I have shared an image that came to me that seemed to have no meaning, and they ended up gleaning something meaningful from it. Ultimately, this is also useful to their therapeutic process.

■ **Exercise 6.6: Remembering the Vision of Yourself as a Healer**

After releasing our fears, we need to fill ourselves back up. For those of us who have heard the call to be a healer, it is important to reconnect with our original vision—what called us to our professions in the first place. In this exercise you will be infusing a touchstone or talisman (see Exercise 4.10 on creating a touchstone or talisman) with that original vision of yourself. The touchstone can be used to remind yourself of who you really are as a healer or health care professional.

Refer to Appendix C for general instructions for grounding and visualization exercises.

While holding your touchstone in one of your hands, begin by connecting with your breath; remember to take the breath deep into your heart. Take about two minutes to do this.

As you continue to breathe, begin to move your consciousness along with your breath down into your heart, into your center of love, joy, and compassion. Notice what your heart center looks and feels like, including such characteristics as color, temperature, structure, tone, and quality. Just as there are many types of fear, so too are there many facets to the heart chakra. Explore yours. Stay with this for about three to five minutes.

From the heart center, allow your consciousness to drift back to a time when you knew you wanted to be or felt called to be a healer. It does not matter how far back in time you go, but the clearer the image, the more potent it will be for you. Remember the intention—the reasons you wanted to be a healer. If your reasons seem shallow or fear-based, let them fall away, and go deeper into the memory, until you reach the true reason for the calling. Allow yourself to move fully into the image of you in that moment of love, caring, and compassion; wear it like a cloak. See and feel yourself in the image; be the image. Feel the desire and the certainty coursing through your body, filling every muscle, every cell, every atom with your intent. See yourself expanding in order to contain all the energy of love, caring, and compassion for your fellow human beings. Work with this image for two to three minutes.

When you feel ready, remember your touchstone and let it become a container for your experience. Pour all your experience of your love, caring, and compassion into your touchstone until it's overflowing; notice that you do not empty in the process. Continue filling yourself and your touchstone for two to three minutes.

When you are ready, follow your breath back up and out into the world.

For those of you who are medical doctors, it may also be useful to reconnect with the Hippocratic oath (see Appendix E). The last two lines are: "While I continue to keep this Oath unviolated, may it be granted to me to enjoy life and the practice of the art, respected by all men, in all times. But should I trespass and violate this Oath, may the reverse be my lot." I can't help but wonder if the increasing distrust in and disdain for medical doctors reflect some perceived "trespass" against the oath.

*It's more than just words
that got spoken,
there was the language
of the heart.*

—DAVID WILCOX,
LANGUAGE OF THE HEART

■ **Exercise 6.7: Coming from Your Heart**

Whether or not you can recall a time of knowing that you just had to be a healer, and whether or not your game plan is provided by a middle manager, you can always choose to come from your heart. What does this mean? It means acting as if you were fully able to come from a place of love or compassion for each one of your patients at all times. And it means treating that middle manager with love and compassion too. How do you do this? Refer to Exercises 4.12–4.18, 5.3, and 5.6. Also see sidebar Radiating Love on page 100.

The Story of INDOC

In interviewing people for this book, I came across Tom LaGrelius, the founder of INDOC (Independent Doctors of the South Los Angeles Bay Area), a medical doctor who demonstrates what one person can do when he remembers who he really is and why he chose his profession.

Tom started practicing medicine with a group of highly respected physicians in 1974, the year the HMO law was passed, mandating the presence of HMOs in every company that had more than 100 employees. Tom watched as his group was adversely affected by this trend, while a local HMO just kept growing. Tom's group, except for Tom, voted to contract with this HMO. Because Tom was the clinic coordinator and chairman of the executive committee at the time, he was responsible for negotiating the contract. "I could feel it in my bones that it was a bad idea," he remembers, "so I kept asking for all kinds of things . . . [including] a seat on the board." Tom, who was not a stockholder, was told that he could go to the meetings but could not vote. "I started going to . . . board meetings, and they were horrible," he comments. At the last meeting Tom attended, the board voted to set up a series of "artificial barriers" that would prevent patients from getting their hernias fixed for at least six months, and by that time they would be out of the group's HMO and thus become someone else's liability. Tom says, "I sat in the corner, waiting for any one of these physicians . . . to raise their hands and say, 'You know, it . . . wouldn't really be very nice of us to do that, kind of contrary to the ethics that we swore as physicians." But no one did.

Tom went back to his group and explained the situation. "You know, we agreed when we did this that if we saw this type of thing going on we'd have to bail out because it wouldn't be proper, and so I'm telling you it's unethical, it's wrong, it's disgusting, and we've got to get out." But the money was too much for his colleagues to give up. Tom continued to practice with the group for a while, but he refused to take any HMO patients or money. Eventually he was forced out, and the situation repeated itself a few years later.

Tom started building his own group of like-minded physicians who were willing to give up their HMO contracts in order to have the freedom to run their practices as they saw fit. They started advertising to those people who didn't have insurance or who were dissatisfied with their insurance, and to employers who were being treated badly by their HMOs. INDOC became a great success. Tom observes, "There was never any question of what to do, it was just a matter of whether you had the intestinal fortitude or the moral gumption to do it, or whether you were willing to suffer lower income, or whether you were willing to go out and give speeches and market your own practice and just try to spread the word. I got more active in medical politics, which I really wasn't interested in before, but it seemed necessary. And now the whole picture has changed; we have really changed the perception in the medical community."

Tom considers himeself "about the most visible doctor in California." He explains, "My home number is published, and my office phone forwards to my cell. That's how you treat patients well. And why don't other doctors do that? I still have a wonderful life. Do you realize how much easier it is for me to answer a telephone call than to pick up a beeper, read the number, call back an exchange, talk to the exchange, get the telephone number to call, identify the person, and call them back?"

When asked if fear was a motivating factor in all the changes he made in his life and practice, Tom says, "I like to think I'm not motivated by fear." But he agrees that managed care itself seems to engender fear and greed. "Fear and greed have been the two motivations that have allowed physicians to get into these messes. . . . One thing that has characterized my practice is that at every turn in the road I always said, 'No, it's wrong.' And everybody thought I was nuts. 'You're never going to make it, you're never going to survive. You can't survive without these things anymore. You're going to lose your entire practice.' Well, I never lost my entire practice. I had to change; I had to market myself. I had to do things to stay alive, but . . . to me it always felt like you have two alternatives: you can violate your Hippocratic oath and become morally bankrupt, or you can choose another route."

There are now several INDOC organizations in California, with other similar organizations springing up around the country to provide services at reduced costs to patients who pay out of pocket.

Oh, that's God; he thinks he's a doctor.

—PUNCH LINE OF A LATE TWENTIETH-CENTURY JOKE

"With the advent of managed care, the unbelievable hassles, the disrespect, the attack on professional dignity, the attack on the doctor-patient relationship, the enormous amount of unnecessary paperwork," [Harold Eist, psychiatrist, Bethesda, Maryland] *said in a recent interview, many doctors "are so depressed and stressed that instead of going back to work, they're just saying, 'I'm not going to bang my head against the wall."*

"The public should be concerned," he said, because "it is not in the interest of society to have a demoralized population of healers."

—DAVID S. HILZENRATH, "PHYSICIANS ARE LEAVING JOBS TO COLLECT DISABILITY BENEFITS," THE *WASHINGTON POST*, FEBRUARY 23, 1998

Modal Hospital

"Ninety percent of what I did there came from love and compassion, and that's no longer valued. They took the heart right out of us," says Diana, one of the health care workers who comprised a special adolescent/young adult treatment team at Modal Hospital (a fictional name). One of the hospital's stated goals was to provide such excellent, patient-centered care that no one, patient or staff, would ever consider going elsewhere. For a long time it lived up to that goal: "For about twelve years everybody stayed, there was almost no attrition." During that time the atmosphere was about as healing as anyone, patient or staff, could wish for: it had heart and joy, lightness and play, compassion and caring.

"When I first started there, we had two nurses on every shift, which allowed us to be creative," Diana comments. "We could talk, and try new things. It was like a home away from home. I never left on time. I would do my nurturing work [with the patients] and then, when the next shift came on, I would start to do my paperwork.

"We as a staff felt like we were being taken care of and our needs were being met, [so] we were able to be more generous. I remember when I started there was a tradition of writing cards to people on the staff. 'Just to let you know, we're thinking about you.' And we would all sign the cards and give them to the people. Or if somebody was graduating, we handed a graduation card to him. And if we heard that someone's parent had died, we would send her a sympathy card. One of our staff members whose birthday fell on her day off actually came in that day because, she said,

'Where else would I want to be on my birthday but with the people I'm closest to?'

"It was a very loving environment. People really cared about one another. We used to work as a team, which included the patient and their identified support people. . . . Things were created specifically for a particular client or situation, and everybody pitched in. We tried to figure out which one among us had the best rapport [with a particular patient] and we would let them be the team leader. There was considerable appreciation for what each team member brought to the meetings. There was an honoring."

But then the hospital began to change. What had been a place of healing became a business, an investment in someone's portfolio. Program directors found themselves in the position of middle management having to respond to upper management's demands to cut costs. Not knowing what else to do and fearing for their jobs, they started cutting other positions.

Diana continues, "Fear just brought more fear and more paranoia, and the mistreatment of people—staff and patients alike. There was this huge fear that anyone leaving would be angry and thinking of sabotage. After I decided to leave and had given my two weeks' notice, I came in and was told I didn't need to stay the day, even though I had patients scheduled."

She finishes, "We used to have continuity; a person could start with a particular team member as an inpatient, then move to outpatient and they would keep the same contact person. When this changed, people got lost. And if they just stopped calling and didn't schedule their follow-up appointments, nobody called them to check and ask, 'Are things okay? Do you need to come in?' There wasn't that follow-up anymore."

Fear can destroy even the greatest programs. It didn't happen at Modal overnight, but the moment it began it devastated the staff and impacted the patients, who were sometimes witness to the mistreatment of the staff. And one year after the massive layoff, human resources started hiring new people, acknowledging they had made a big mistake in letting go of all the employees.

This story suggests that organizations, like people, need to be cognizant of the fear in the system. Organizers must take time to address that fear consciously, so that decisions can be made from a position of strength and love rather than weakness and fear. Because organizations are made up of people, each of us must be willing to take responsibility for his or her own fears, and we must name the fears we see in the system. This can be terrifying, especially for companies that are large and have many layers of management, which can seem very impersonal. Remember that the person above you is a human being who is probably just as scared as you. Try coming to that person from a heart space. (See the Exercises for Cultivating Heart Energy (pages 84–89), as well as Exercise 5.6.)

EXERCISES FOR ADJUNCT AND ALLIED HEALTH CARE PROFESSIONALS

This means you! I believe that all individuals involved in the health care profession—educators, insurance adjusters, reporters, advertisers, public relations firms, and managers of HMOs—are contributors to the field of fear in the system. As such, they are responsible for the experience of fear in the people who enter that system for assistance, and in the people who are supposed to be caring for them. They are also responsible for the toll that fear takes on our ability to heal.

Just as patients and providers need to take responsibility for their own fears, you must take responsibility for any personal fears that may contribute to the field of fear in health care. But how can you take responsibility for those fears?

Begin by recognizing those fears. Then try speaking up about what you have recognized. In this way, you refuse to participate in any fear-mongering. You might also actively seek to instill other values in your industry. For example, if you are a reporter, you could do a story on the positive, healing effects of compassion. If you are an insurance adjuster, you could learn about the new ways of handling worker's compensation insurance. If you are a CEO of an HMO, you could survey your shareholders to see if they would be willing to make less on their investment if it meant that more patients would be well served. If you are part of an ad agency that works for a pharmaceutical company, you could highlight the benefits of the medication in your materials, rather than emphasizing what will happen to the patient if he doesn't use the product. If you are an educator, you could decide that none of the students on your watch is going to be taught by intimidation.

I've included a few stories in this section that should help you recognize some of the fears in the system and inspire you to take personal responsibility for transforming what you can. We are all in this together. It is obvious that our health care system needs revamping. Certainly there are fiduciary and other "real," external issues that need to be faced. But if we go back to the introduction and review Wilber's four-quadrant model (see page 17), we will see that there are other internal factors to consider, with the heart perhaps chief among them.

Being Heard:
A Health Care Student Speaks Out

Diane, whom we met in the sidebar Patty's Sneakers (pages 78–80), is a student in a nurse-midwife program. I asked her to talk about the fears she has been aware of during the course of her health care education. She has noticed that there is a lot of fear in student health care providers—"fear of the system, fear of looking dumb." She thinks one of the most important things to allay such fears is "to know that one's questions will be appreciated." Diane emphasizes that students don't just want to be heard superficially, but received as though the listener really understood how important that question was—as though no question could possibly be dumb.

This is extremely important, since the student practitioner, and later the doctor, will treat her patients as she has been treated. Diane says, "I remember last spring, while doing my medical-surgical rotation, I was disgusted by the way medical residents and interns responded to medical students' questions with silence. They would simply stare at the student who had asked the question, as if to say, 'That question isn't even good enough for me to answer.'" Diane had her own taste of this. "I often sensed exasperation and incredulity on the part of my instructors who thought that I was asking 'too many' questions. In both medical and nursing programs, questions are discouraged because of fear."

Not surprisingly, Diane most appreciates instructors and supervisors who not only tolerate her questions, but also treat them as truly important. This helps her overcome her fears and self-doubt, allowing her to be more fully present with her patients, rather than worry about the question that wasn't answered. And because she is not treated as stupid for asking something, she can more easily pass the information and behavior on to her patients.

Note that Diane is at the top of her class; asking questions makes a difference. Studies also show that students who study together, asking questions of each other and sharing knowledge, tend to score higher on tests than the "lone wolves."

Karin's School

After a personal healing success, Karin was excited about complementary medical disciplines; she felt certain this was what she was meant to do with her life. She studied abroad for several years and eventually developed her own very successful practice in the United States. But Karin felt that this wasn't enough; she couldn't see all the prospective clients herself, so she started a school. By all accounts, the school was a success: Karin's students were thrilled with their educational experience, and many more people were well served by the school's graduates.

But none of this mattered, it seemed, to the government—there were rules, after all, and hoops to jump through. After a couple of years of trying to comply with the rules, which seemed to change from moment to moment and which seemed designed to make it impossible to ever do anything out of the medical norm, Karin thought it was all going to come together. Hoping for the best, she expanded the school, taking on an enormous debt in the process. Within a month, she received a letter saying that her school was being shut down.

Karin was very afraid, angry, and sad. In addition, many others would be disappointed and hurt, both emotionally and financially. She took a day off to consider her options. At the end of the day she had come to a place of peace and new possibilities and felt ready to move on. The next day she received a phone call from a government official-who had had a dream, after which she was convinced that Karin's school had to be supported. The woman said, "You are exactly what the state should be licensing, but what was running us was fear—fear of new things, unknown things, things not understood, things that couldn't be put in the old box." True to her word, this woman helped Karin get the license she needed to continue providing her students with the education they wanted.

7
Making Friends
with Death

Death is a part of the whole cycle of life, and it is probably the biggest contributor to the field of fear in health care—and possibly in our culture as a whole. We fight against it, physicians fight against it, we spend enormous energy and health care dollars fighting against it, and yet it comes to us all. Though it is imperative for each person to work with this fear, I do not have any specific suggestions for doing so; even religious and spiritual leaders seem unable to alleviate this deepest fear, which expresses itself uniquely in each individual.

> *An idea of health that does not generously and gracefully accommodate the fact of death is obviously incomplete.*
>
> —WENDELL BERRY,
> *LIFE IS A MIRACLE: AN ESSAY AGAINST MODERN SUPERSTITION*

For me, the release from the fear of death came as an unexpected grace—one day the fear was there, the next day it was gone. In the middle of an anxiety attack prompted by fears of death, I picked up a book[1] that had been sitting by my bedside for six months. Even before opening it, I felt waves and waves of peace wash over me. Perhaps it was all the years of personal work finally coming together; perhaps it was the beauty of the author of the book, who transcended his own death to grant me peace. Many people don't realize this peace until death is actually near. But perhaps the answer is simply to face it like any other fear—acknowledge it, work with it, release it, and find something to replace it.[2]

Bernadette's Story: Facing Death in Childbirth

This is one woman's story about her experience with various fears, including the fear of death, during the process of giving birth to her two children. Her story is not everybody's; it is hers. But it is a good example of how to deal with this fear.

Bernadette had two very different pregnancies and births. The first was easy, and Bernadette knew the baby was safe the whole time. The fears she carried had more to do with her own performance anxiety—would she be able to do what was necessary in the birthing process?—and the kind of welcome her daughter would receive when she appeared.

"I was concerned—would there be fear present at her birth?" remembers Bernadette. She saw herself as her daughter's spiritual guardian, responsible for protecting her psychic space at birth. This was what ultimately made her choose a home birth, so that she could control the environment into which her daughter was born. What Bernadette wanted more than anything was for her child to be born into a field of love, something she thought was missing in her prenatal encounters at her clinic.

Bernadette's second pregnancy was much different. She decided early on to have another home birth because of the beauty and richness of her first experience. But she experienced inner fears almost immediately during her second pregnancy. She characterizes them as "the traditional fears that mothers-to-be have—that something's going to be wrong with their baby, that something's going to go wrong, that something's already gone wrong, or that something's just not quite right, but you can't put your finger on it."

Though her first response to the fear was to "check out and try to ignore it," Bernadette began working consciously with her fears. She found physical support in various kinds of bodywork and discovered that she could "breathe into" some of the unconscious lingering fears from her first labor and let them move through and out of her body. She also recognized the need to admit her fears to her husband and ask him for help. "Then it really shifted, and the second trimester was very different."

In her second trimester, Bernadette's fears had to do with misinformation—inaccuracies that were recorded in her chart and could have jeopardized her plans for a home birth. Though the midwives eventually caught all the mistakes, Bernadette had to live with the fear for several days each time.

In the third trimester, the fears were about the baby's heart tones, which began to dip. Heart tones are the sounds made by heart valves opening and closing during each heart-beat; this is the "lubb-dupp" that you hear when you put your ear against someone else's chest. Bernadette resolutely held on to the plan for a home birth, knowing that some people would consider her crazy for doing so. In fact, she says, "We got kicked out [of our clinic] in the ninth month of prenatal care. They told us we couldn't see midwives [for our check-ups] if we were doing a home birth; we had to see a doctor. So there I am, naked on the examination table, and she comes in and tells me, 'I'm sorry, we can't care for you.'"

Bernadette chalked this up to the clinic's fear of liability problems. Her husband panicked at the news but she remained calm, telling him, "We have to focus on the baby; we have no extra energy to get caught up in that fear. Stay on track." She was convinced that she could have this baby at home, so she found another clinic that would support her decision. "Had we gone into fear and let that run the decisions throughout the whole pregnancy, then we would have done a hospital birth, and the birth would have been very different; it probably would have been a C-section."

Bernadette points out that either choice would have yielded a safe, albeit very different, delivery. But she believes that "if there's fear and there might be a problem, then you should go where those fears are going to be calmed." For her, calm came from processing the fear and listening deeply to the baby in her womb. "If I hadn't done that, we would have gone and gotten more tests and done a lot more medical intervention, and rather than helping, in . . . our case, it would have fueled the fear more and it would have altered the course of all our decisions to follow. We would have been listening to the information outside of ourselves rather than what we needed to keep listening to, which was the baby, who was talking to us and the midwives. That's hard to do. When you're in such a vulnerable place you just want to go to an expert and say, 'Tell me what to do.'"

Shortly before her due date, Bernadette had a friend come over to listen to her as she named all of the fears she had been through during the pregnancy. "I just wanted to say out loud—to someone who could witness it—what the fears were, because I hadn't really done that. I hadn't wanted to talk about them too much because I didn't want to give them more power, so a lot of them I dealt with on my own during the pregnancy. As I'd be lying in bed at night . . . I would do my own thing where I would visualize the fear getting smaller, and my power getting greater; maybe surround [the fear] in light, or send it away."

Bernadette feels strongly that all of this work allowed her to deal with what eventually came: a turning point during her labor when she needed to decide whether to remain at home or be transported to the hospital. "I think if I hadn't faced the fears all along, worked with them and gotten help and support, transformed them, and used them as a catalyst they would have all come up in that split second. It could have clouded everything then. But I knew exactly what I needed to do, [to go to the hospital in the middle of labor], and exactly what help I needed to ask for inside myself and outside myself. I have never been so clear in my life. [In the hospital] I was saying [to the doctors and nurses and midwives], 'I need you to do this, and you to do this.' I would go into the letting go, and I would come out and . . . it was like being in charge and out of control at the same time. When it's a life-or-death choice you really want to be able to call on that ability."

Bernadette is really in touch with her own inner wisdom, and she uses it along with external information to create her own birthing experiences. She regularly works with and breathes through any fears that arise in order to keep coming back to herself. This power is available to us all, especially with the love and support or simple witnessing of others.

After listening deeply, Bernadette followed her instinct with such certainty that her requests or commands were followed, even in the emergency room of a hospital where the voice of the physician is usually sacrosanct. While not all of us will be able to achieve the level of confidence and decisiveness of Bernadette, particularly in the face of a scary situation, we can look to her as an example. And we can use her as an ally in our visualizations, as we imagine those who have gone before us.

AN EXERCISE FOR WOMEN

Women in Western cultures have been taught to fear their bodies and their childbearing capabilities. These abilities and everything associated with them have been turned into medical conditions rather than natural functions. Menstrual periods have been called "the curse," and we are taught to expect pain and discomfort from them. We are derided and paid less at our jobs because we may be unable to function at peak capacity when we are having our periods or during pregnancy and for some time thereafter. We are then taught to fear the end of our childbearing years because we will look old and withered, and because we will no longer have any "purpose" in life. (See the sidebar Fear and the Media on page 20.)

My thesis was that the fear of death is so predominant in the origins of modern medicine that it becomes a barrier to moving into any new models.

—LOIS, A FORMER HOSPITAL ADMINISTRATOR

In addition to these cultivated fears, pregnancy and childbirth bring us face to face with our most primal fear—the fear of death, which I believe ultimately underscores most of the other fears in our health care system. Though many of us like to think of pregnancy and childbirth as completely natural and safe, the truth is that creating life is a complicated, mysterious process that does not always have the anticipated or desired outcome; either the mother or the child or both can die in the process.

If I'm afraid of death, then I will become extremely cautious and worried in life, since something might happen to me. So the more I fear death the more I fear life, and the less I live.

—TREYA WILBER, *GRACE AND GRIT*

It is best to begin young in cultivating an attitude of gratitude for this awesome, terrifying, and miraculous gift of creativity and power that our bodies possess—as well as for the new freedom and creativity we enter into when the physical birthing potential leaves us. Showing our daughters this attitude is imperative, and cultivating it in ourselves as adults is tremendously beneficial. I had just achieved a feeling of joy and gratitude at the point when my menses began to leave me; I wish I could have done that sooner.

■ **Exercise 7.1: Making Friends with Our Menstrual Cycles**

Take the opportunity of each menses (or, for those of you who either have stopped bleeding or haven't yet started, each full moon) to reflect on at least one reason why you are grateful to have a body that is or has been capable of giving birth—with all the awesome power, responsibility, joy, creativity, pain, and fear this ability brings with it, including the fear of death.

AN EXERCISE FOR MEN

I am not aware of a life experience for men that is similar to the woman's menstrual cycle, except perhaps the process of aging. One of the great clichés of our culture is the older man who seeks out the company of a much younger woman, presumably to deny the fact of aging and the underlying fear of death.

I haven't resolved my own fear of death, but what I have learned from Jim [Brigham] is how to sit with someone, just sit with them while death walks in the room. I wonder what it will be like to be a doctor who doesn't see death as the enemy.

—MAREN R. MONSEN, M.D.,
FROM THE DOCUMENTARY
THE VANISHING LINE

■ Exercise 7.2: Making Friends with Your Life Cycles

Take the opportunity once a month, perhaps at the new moon, to reflect on at least one reason why you are grateful to be the age you are right now, with the body that you have right now—a body that may show the wear and tear in its wrinkles and sore muscles but also reflects the life wisdom you have achieved. Be sure to acknowledge your sadness and fears, especially that of dying, as well as your triumphs and joys.

FOR HEALTH CARE PRACTITIONERS ONLY: MAKING FRIENDS WITH THE CYCLE OF LIFE IN YOUR PATIENTS

My medical training focused on procedures, not on how to talk with patients about their death. An uncomfortable thought was creeping into my mind: was the problem just my training, or was it my own terror of looking death in the face?

—JIM BRIGHAM,
FROM THE DOCUMENTARY
THE VANISHING LINE

Making friends with the cycle of life obviously includes accepting death. But I think Jim Brigham, a social worker who worked with patients facing death, is correct when he says that the difficulty he had in talking with dying patients was in large part due to his own unresolved fears of death. The answer for you, as for everyone, is to do your own work with your fear.

Though I feel as though I have made my own peace with death, occasionally I still find myself in a place of, if not fear, apprehension mixed with curiosity. It is a great mystery, after all. And, as with so many aspects of the journey, my relationship with this momentous one changes as I change, sometimes from moment to moment.

I recently told a friend that I sometimes feel like an impostor: here I am, publishing a book on healing without fear and leading workshops on the same topic, when I often lapse into fear as my first response. But that is what acute fear is for—alerting me to possible danger and then, hopefully, subsiding. I find that it does subside ever more quickly, as I take my own and others' advice to pause, breathe, reflect, and try something new. May it work as well for you, that we might all release the mantle of chronic fear that currently seems to cloak our health care system.

Namaste.

Appendix A:
Iron John Interpreted

In this section I look at the story of Iron John as if it were a dream of mine. I view all of the characters in the story as parts of myself.

I begin with the premise that Iron John is my shadow—the parts of myself, "good" or "bad," that I have relegated to the deepest, darkest place in the forest. I have done this out of fear of the loss of love from those around me, because the parts I have banished are the aspects of myself that others find unacceptable. Yet this banishment happens as if by magic; initially I am not even aware that it has happened.

My first awareness comes when I notice that more and more parts of myself are disappearing into the forest—parts that can and should provide me with sustenance. Once I notice this, I search for those lost parts and end up losing more, as if the shadow is now a black hole sucking more of me into it. Now I won't even go searching anymore. This is where I might acknowledge that fear has something to do with the problem, though I do not use the word *fear*. In fact, the word is not even mentioned until the stranger—someone outside me, such as a friend, a therapist, or an aspect of myself I have not yet encountered—names the problem for me by saying that he is never stopped by fear. So the "fearless" one goes into the woods for me and finds the wild, hairy man at the bottom of the pool. The stranger does not go into the forest alone, however. He takes his dog, his instinctual, animal self, with him. The dog shows the hunter where Iron John lives, because the feelings and issues we relegate to the woods are quite often related to our animal, instinctual natures, as opposed to our enculturated selves.

I bring my shadow up out of the pool and the forest of my unconscious and take it back to the castle where I can observe it but keep it safely locked up so I don't have to deal with my fear directly. I can address my anger, outrage, or sadness instead, because this is a rather pathetic creature that now stands before me. It is the king, or masculine part of me, that locks up the shadow and then gives the key to the queen, or the feminine part of me, for safekeeping. (In dreams, kings often represent our enculturated selves, while queens are usually more closely connected with nature and our instinctual selves.) The queen puts the key under her pillow, the place where she lays her head at night when she goes to sleep. Thus, Iron John is once again relegated to the unconscious.

The situation would probably stay this way forever if it weren't for my youthful, lively, exuberant son, the other part of me who, like the stranger, seems to have no fear of Iron John. It is also the part of me that is still closest to my "golden" self, my soul, in the form of a golden ball. He holds the golden ball in his hands and plays with it. (Adults tend to hold precious items too close, locking them up—as Iron John is locked up—for safekeeping rather than bringing them out for play.) The golden ball eventually, necessarily, bounces into Iron John's cage. This is a clue to his real nature and value. But Iron John will not return the ball to my youthful self until I set him free, and I finally let him go because this part of me knows the value of my soul.

But having released my shadow, I suddenly remember my fear of being reprimanded by my father and I call out to the shadow, asking him not to go. He comes back, but knows that if he stays he will be caged again. So he scoops me up and takes me back to the forest with him, where I begin to learn more about my true nature. I also learn about his true nature, which is nothing to be afraid of and actually has much to teach and offer me. In fact, it is through his gifts that I am eventually able to defeat the other king's enemies (perhaps those who would censure me), win the hand of my beloved (thus integrating my masculine and feminine aspects), who has known my identity all along, and be reunited with the rest of my family—my whole self—including Iron John, who finally appears as his kingly self and puts all of his and my wealth at my disposal. And what wealth it is; in Wilber's terms (see page 17) it includes our internal ways of knowing.

Appendix B:
The Art of Dialoguing

Dialoguing is just what it sounds like: having a conversation. But this is an imaginary conversation you have with an aspect of yourself, such as the part of you that is afraid. You can dialogue on paper, with different colors of ink for each "voice," or by labeling each voice as it speaks.

You can also dialogue aloud using the "empty chair" technique. Many people find this style much easier. Sit down opposite an empty chair. Imagine that a part of yourself is sitting in that chair. Start off by saying hi and then asking some simple questions. Or launch into a discussion of how you are feeling and why you wanted to talk. Relax, and allow your imagination to supply the responses, as though they were coming from another person. You might want to use a tape recorder or have someone present who can take notes for you. Frequently, the unconscious is aware of feelings and problems that the conscious mind is not aware of, and these will more easily "appear" when we tap into different parts of ourselves.

For additional ideas, please see Ira Progoff's *At a Journal Workshop*.

Appendix C:
General Instructions for All Grounding and Guided Visualization Exercises

You will experience the most benefits if you can just listen to, rather than read, the visualization instructions included in the main text. Try recording the instructions in your own voice ahead of time or have an ally read them to you as you listen in a state of relaxation. It is sometimes helpful to have an ally available who can help talk you through any stuck places by offering encouragement and providing reminders of what a powerful person you truly are.

It is important to be in a relaxed but alert posture, not so relaxed that you will fall asleep but not so alert that you are uncomfortable. As you listen to the instructions stay connected with your breath, remembering to take the breath deep into your belly, your place of power. Also remember that, just as your breath takes you in and down, it can bring you back up and out as well. So if you find yourself becoming extremely uncomfortable, just follow your breath back up and out into the room.

Appendix D:
The Chakras

A chakra is a "sacred center of the self," a "center of activity that receives, assimilates, and expresses life force energy."[1] There are actually multiple chakra systems, some of which identify hundreds of chakras. The chart below illustrates the most commonly known system, comprising seven main chakras.

First chakra: Located at the base of the spine, this is related to basic survival issues, such as food, shelter, safety, trust, family, and prosperity.

Second chakra: Located in the genitals, it is related to sexuality and creativity.

Third chakra: Located in the solar plexus, it is related to self-esteem, will, and power.

Fourth chakra: Located in the heart, it is related to heart values such as love, joy, compassion, generosity, and relationship; called "the rainbow bridge," it connects the bottom triad (body, earth) with the upper triad (head, spirit); it also connects our hearts with the hearts of others.

Fifth chakra: Located in the throat, it is related to communication and finding our own voices.

Seven Major Chakras

7   Spirit/God connection

6   Insight/intuition

5   Communication

4   Love, joy

3   Power, self-esteem, will

2   Sex, creativity

1   Survival

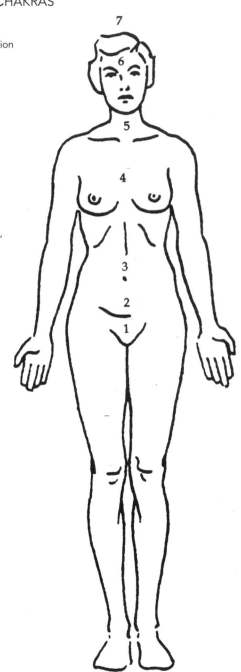

Sixth chakra: Located in the "third eye" (center of the forehead), it is related to the sight found in dreams and intuition.

Seventh chakra: Located in the crown, it is related to our belief systems and our ability to analyze and assimilate information and wisdom; it is usually represented as a lotus (either open or closed), and it is where we connect with our spiritual nature, God, the universe.

Appendix E:
The Oath of Hippocrates

I swear by Apollo the physician and Aesculapius, and Health, and All-heal, and all the gods and goddesses, that, according to my ability and judgment, I will keep this Oath and this stipulation. . . . I will follow that system of regimen which, according to my ability and judgment, I consider for the benefit of my patients, and abstain from whatever is deleterious and mischievous. . . . With purity and with holiness I will pass my life and practice my Art. . . . Into whatever houses I enter, I will go into them for the benefit of the sick, and will abstain from every voluntary act of mischief and corruption. . . . While I continue to keep this Oath unviolated, may it be granted to me to enjoy life and the practice of the art, respected by all men, in all times. But should I trespass and violate this Oath, may the reverse be my lot.

Notes

Introduction

1. Caroline Myss, *Why People Don't Heal and How They Can* (Three Rivers, Mich.: Three Rivers Press, 1998).

2. *The Hundredth Monkey and Other Paradigms of the Paranormal* Kendrick Frazier, ed., (Amherst, N.Y.: Prometheus Books, 1991).

3. Rupert Sheldrake, *The Presence of the Past: Morphic Resonance and the Habits of Nature* (New York: Vintage Books, 1988), viii.

4. Ibid, 108.

5. Innate Intelligence, "Who and What is Network Chiropractic?" *Network Chiropractic Newsletter* 1, no. 4 (1993): 1.

6. Adapted from Ken Wilber, *A Theory of Everything* (Boston: Shambhala, 2000).

7. Barry Glassner, *The Culture of Fear: Why Americans Are Afraid of the Wrong Things* (New York: Basic Books, 1999).

8. S. E. Asch, "Studies of Independence and Submission to Group Pressure: I. A Minority of One Against a Unanimous Majority," *Psychological Monographs* 70, no. 417 (1956).

Chapter 1

1. During the course of writing this book, I came across this acronym several times, but I do not know the original source. My apologies and gratitude to whoever created it.

2. See Lauren Artress, *Walking a Sacred Path: Rediscovering the Labyrinth as a Spiritual Tool* (New York: Riverhead Books, 1995).

3. For more information on birth order, please see the Ohio State University Extension Fact Sheet on Birth Order at http://ohioline.osu.edu/hyg-fact/5000/5279.html; and Clifford Isaacson and Kris Radish, *The Birth Order Effect* (Avon, Mass.: Adams Media Corporation, 2002).

4. See Robert H. Hopcke, *A Guided Tour of the Collected Works of C. G. Jung* (Boston: Shambhala, 1989).

Chapter 2

1. See Arnold Mindell, *Dreambody: The Body's Role in Revealing the Self* (Santa Monica: Sigo Press, 1982).

Chapter 3

1. See Arnold Mindell, *Working on Yourself Alone: Inner Dreambody Work* (London: Arkana, 1990). See also Ron Kurtz, *Body-Centered Psychotherapy: The Hakomi Method* (Mendocino, Calif.: LifeRhythm, 1990).

2. See Herbert Benson and Miriam Z. Klipper, *The Relaxation Response* (New York: Avon, 1975).

3. This affirmation was adapted from Joy Drake and Kathy Tyler, *The Transformation Game* (Stamford, Conn.: U.S. Games Systems, 1987).

4. See Joshua Piven and David Borgenicht, *The Worst-Case Scenario Survival Handbook* (San Francisco: Chronute Books LLC, 1999).

Chapter 4

1. See Andrew Weil, M.D., *8 Weeks to Optimum Health* (New York: Alfred A. Knopf, 1997).

2. See Valerie V. Hunt, *Infinite Mind: The Science of Human Vibrations* (Malibu, Calif.: Malibu Publishing Co., 1989).

3. Adapted from Anodea Judith, *Eastern Body, Western Mind: Psychology and the Chakra System as a Path to the Self* (Berkeley, Calif.: Celestial Arts, 1996).

4. Hunt, *Infinite Mind: The Science of Human Vibrations.*

5. See GAIAM's Pilates videocassettes with Ana Caban.

6. See Dr. Peter J. D'Adamo and Catherine Whitney, *Eat Right 4 Your Type* (New York: G. P. Putnam's Sons, 1996).

7. See Iona Marsaa Teeguarden, *The Joy of Feeling: Bodymind Acupressure—Jin Shin Do* (Tokyo: Japan Publications, 1987), 81.

8. Ibid.

9. See Benson and Klipper, *The Relaxation Response.*

10. See the movie *Harvey* for another example of an ally. Produced by Universal Studios. Directed by Henry Koster. 104 minutes. Universal International Pictures, 1950. Videocassette.

11. Adapted from Mantak Chia, *Awaken Healing Energy Through the Tao* (Santa Fe: Aurora Press, 1983).

12. Gregg Braden, *The Isaiah Effect: Decoding the Lost Science of Prayer and Prophecy* (New York: Harmony Books, 2000).

Chapter 5

1. See Harriet Beinfield and Efrem Korngold *Between Heaven and Earth: A Guide to Chinese Medicine* (New York: Ballantine Books, 1991).

2. Based on my work with Ken Cohen.

3. See John Fox, *Finding What You Didn't Lose: Expressing Your Truth and Creativity Through Poem-Making* (New York: G. P. Putnam's Sons, 1995), and Julia Cameron and Mark Bryan, *The Artist's Way: A Spiritual Path to Higher Creativity* (New York: G. P. Putnam's Sons, 1992).

4. See *Into the Woods*, a play by Stephen Sondheim based on these fairy tales. Produced by Image Entertainment. Directed by James Lapine. 151 minutes. Image Entertainment, 1991. Videocassette.

5. See Marie Cardinal, *The Words to Say It* (Cambridge, Mass: VanVactor and Goodheart, 1983).

6. See Susan Chernak McElroy, *Animals as Guides for the Soul* (New York: Ballantine Publishing Group, 1998), and Francis Melville, *The Book of Angels* (Hauppauge, N.Y.: Barron's, 2001).

7. See Robert A. Johnson, *Inner Work: Using Dreams and Active Imagination for Personal Growth* (San Francisco: Harper & Row, 1986).

8. From Sogyal Rinpoche, *The Tibetan Book of Living and Dying* (San Francisco: HarperSanFrancisco, 1992), 193.

9. See Larry Dossey, M.D., *Healing Words:The Power of Prayer and the Practice of Medicine* (San Francisco: HarperSanFrancisco, 1993).

10. Ibid.

11. Ibid.

12. See Barbara Metz and John Burchill, *The Enneagram and Prayer* (Nashville, Tenn.: Dimension Books, 1987).

13. Eva Pierrakos and Donovan Thesenga, *Surrender to God Within: Pathwork at the Soul Level* (Del Mar, Calif.: Pathwork Press, 1997), 48–50.

14. See Braden, *The Isaiah Effect: Decoding the Lost Science of Prayer and Prophecy.*

Chapter 7

1. The book was Paramahansa Yogananda's *Autobiography of a Yogi* (Los Angeles: Self-Realization Fellowship, 1959).

2. See the movie *Mr. Rice's Secret* for a beautiful portrayal of a teenage boy's encounter with death, and his subsequent coming-of-age journey. Produced by Beau Rogers and David Forrest. Directed by Nicholas Kendall. 93 minutes. New City Productions, 2000. Videocassette.

Appendix D

1. See Judith, *Eastern Body, Western Mind: Psychology and the Chakra System as a Path to the Self.*

Bibliography

Books, Periodicals, and Videocassettes

Artress, Dr. Lauren. *Walking a Sacred Path—Rediscovering the Labyrinth as a Spiritual Tool.* New York: Riverhead Books, 1995. One minister's personal and professional experiences using a labyrinth as a walking meditation for spiritual growth and healing.

Asch, S. E. "Studies of Independence and Submission to Group Pressure: I. A Minority of One Against a Unanimous Majority." *Psychological Monographs* 70, no. 417 (1956). Shows the positive effect that having an ally creates on a person's willingness to speak his or her truth.

Beinfield, Harriet, and Efrem Korngold, *Between Heaven and Earth: A Guide to Chinese Medicine.* New York: Ballantine Books, 1991. A very readable text on this rich and formidable topic.

Benson, Herbert, and Miriam Z. Klipper. *The Relaxation Response.* New York: Avon, 1975. A deceptively simple approach to meditation that bestows remarkable health benefits.

Braden, Gregg. *The Isaiah Effect: Decoding the Lost Science of Prayer and Prophecy.* New York: Harmony Books, 2000. A look at the power of gratitude.

————. *Walking Between the Worlds: The Science of Compassion.* Bellevue, Wash.: Radio Bookstore Press, 1997. Makes the distinction between external technologies (Western medicine) and internal technologies for healing and wholeness.

Brennan, Barbara Ann. *Hands of Light: A Guide to Healing Through the Human Energy Field.* New York: Bantam Books, 1988. References many scientific studies relating to the human electromagnetic field, auras, chakras, and so forth.

Caban, Ana. *Pilates: Beginning Mat Workout.* Produced and directed by Ted Landon. 40 minutes. Gaiam/Living Arts, 2000. Videocassette. Focuses on working the "powerhouse," the solar plexus area, which is so essential to our feelings of strength and power.

Cardinal, Marie. *The Words to Say It.* Cambridge, Mass.: VanVactor and Goodheart, 1983. A book in which a woman's healing journey is jump-started by her merely saying her dreams aloud.

Cameron, Julia, and Mark Bryan. *The Artist's Way: A Spiritual Path to Higher Creativity.* New York: G. P. Putnam's Sons, 1992. Excellent for giving the artist within permission to express himself or herself.

Chia, Mantak. *Awaken Healing Energy Through the Tao.* Santa Fe: Aurora Press, 1983. A description of the complete inner smile exercise, among other exercises.

Childre, Doc Lew. *Freeze Frame.* Boulder Creek, Calif.: Planetary Publications, 1994. Offers a specific technique to "reduce burnout from overload, anxiety and indecision; access free energy; increase personal effectiveness." Also reports on evidence for the internal/external healing effects of heart energy.

Chodron, Pema. *Tonglen: The Path of Transformation.* Halifax: Vajradhatu Publications, 2001. A Buddhist practice for "eating" fear, pain, and suffering of the self and of others.

Cohen, Ken. *Qigong: Traditional Chinese Exercises for Healing Body, Mind, and Spirit.* Produced by Brad Gilbert. Directed by Ken Cohen. 90 minutes. Sounds True Productions, 1996. Videocassette. A fabulous introduction to one style of Qigong.

———. *The Way of Qigong.* New York: Ballantine Books, 1997. A discussion of the history, theory, and practice of Qigong.

D'Adamo, Dr. Peter J., and Catherine Whitney. *Eat Right 4 Your Type.* New York: G. P. Putnam's Sons, 1996. Looks at the most healthy dietary regimens for the various blood types.

Dossey, Larry, M.D. *Healing Words: The Power of Prayer and the Practice of Medicine.* San Francisco: HarperSanFrancisco, 1993. Takes a broad view of prayer and examines its role in the healing process.

Drake, Joy, and Kathy Tyler. *The Transformation Game*. Stamford, Conn.: U.S. Games Systems, 1987. A fun, synchronistic, noncompetitive, interactive board game for exploring a personal question in depth.

Fox, John. *Finding What You Didn't Lose: Expressing Your Truth and Creativity Through Poem-Making*. New York: G. P. Putnam's Sons, 1995. A wonderful book for undoing all the negative beliefs you have about yourself and your ability to express yourself through poetry.

Frazier, Kendrick (ed.), *The Hundredth Monkey: And Other Paradigms of the Paranormal*. Amherst, N.Y.: Prometheus Books, 1991. A classic tale that illustrates Rupert Sheldrake's morphic field theory.

Gawain, Shakti. *Creative Visualization*. New York: Bantam, 1982. A great primer on the uses of guided visualization.

Gilligan, Carol. *In a Different Voice*. Cambridge, Mass.: Harvard University Press, 1993. A discussion of receptive and expressive style differences between women and men.

Glassner, Barry. *The Culture of Fear: Why Americans Are Afraid of the Wrong Things*. New York: Basic Books, 1999. A fascinating look at the culture of fear in America, from road rage to UFO sightings, and the various ways it is propagated.

Hammerschlag, Carl A., M.D., and Howard D. Silverman, M.D. *Healing Ceremonies: Creating Personal Rituals for Spiritual, Emotional, Physical and Mental Health*. New York: Berkley Publishing Group, 1997. A wonderful primer on how to create personal healing ceremonies, complete with lots of examples.

Hopcke, Robert H. *A Guided Tour of the Collected Works of C. G. Jung*. Boston: Shambhala, 1989. An essential and understandable synopsis of Jung's major contributions to the field of psychology.

Hunt, Valerie V. *Infinite Mind: The Science of Human Vibrations*. Malibu, Calif.: Malibu Publishing Co., 1989. Discusses the differences between the brain, mind, thoughts, and consciousness. Also looks at mind (both personal and universal) as a field with varying frequencies and the brain as a recording device.

Innate Intelligence. *Network Chiropractic Newsletter* 1, no. 4 (1993).

Isaacson, Clifford, and Kris Radish. *The Birth Order Effect*. Avon, Mass.: Adams Media Corporation, 2002. Includes a birth order quiz.

Jahnke, Roger. *The Healer Within*. San Francisco: HarperSanFransisco, 1997. How to activate the healer within yourself.

Jealous, James "Healing and the Natural World," *Alternative Therapies* (January 1997). A healer's personal experience with the influence of fear and its resolution on the healing process.

Johnson, Robert A. *Inner Work: Using Dreams and Active Imagination for Personal Growth*. San Francisco: Harper & Row, 1986. An excellent primer on dream work, active imagination, and ritual.

Judith, Anodea. *Eastern Body, Western Mind: Psychology and the Chakra System as a Path to the Self*. Berkeley, Calif.: Celestial Arts, 1996. Correlates the chakras with character structures and offers exercises for each chakra and personality type.

Jung, Carl Gustav. *Psychological Types*, Collected Works Vol. 6. Princeton, N.J.: Princeton University Press, 1966. Jung's theory about differing psychological types and their strengths and weaknesses.

Kurtz, Ron. *Body-Centered Psychotherapy: The Hakomi Method*. Mendocino, Calif.: LifeRhythm, 1990. An excellent description of a body-centered therapy that can be practiced on oneself.

Levine, Peter A., and Ann Frederick. *Waking the Tiger: Healing Trauma*. Berkeley, Calif.: North Atlantic Books, 1997. Addresses the issue of chronic fear as a thwarted fight-or-flight response that has become frozen in the body.

Lowen, Alexander, M.D. *Fear of Life*. New York: Macmillan Publishing Company, 1980. Discusses how to resolve fears without changing the characteristics that make you a unique person.

McElroy, Susan Chernak. *Animals as Guides for the Soul*. New York: Ballantine Publishing Group, 1998. Using animals as "spirit guides."

Melville, Francis. *The Book of Angels*. Hauppauge, N.Y.: Barron's, 2001. Using angels as "spirit guides."

Mindell, Arnold. *Dreambody: The Body's Role in Revealing the Self*. Santa Monica: Sigo Press, 1982. Mindell's first book on body-centered therapy.

———. *Working on Yourself Alone: Inner Dreambody Work*. London: Arkana, 1990. A good body-centered way to do personal work.

Mines, Stephanie. "Craniosynostosis: Watching Change Overcome Fear." *Massage Bodywork: Nurturing Body, Mind & Spirit* (February/March 1999). A personal experience with fear in the health care system that demonstrates the power of having an ally.

Myss, Caroline. *Why People Don't Heal and How They Can*. Three Rivers, Mich.: Three Rivers Press, 1998.

Pearsall, Paul. *The Heart's Code: Tapping the Wisdom and Power of Our Heart Energy*. New York: Broadway Books, 1998. Considers the role of cellular memories in the mind-body-spirit connection.

Pierrakos, Eva, and Donovan Thesenga. *Surrender to God Within—Pathwork at the Soul Level*. Del Mar, Calif.: Pathwork Press, 1997. Part of the Pathwork series, a guide to a particular spiritual practice.

Piven, Joshua, and David Borgenicht. *The Worst-Case Scenario Survival Handbook*. San Francisco: Chronute Books LLC, 1999. It is not entirely clear whether this book is a spoof of our fear-driven culture or not; in either case, its phenomenal sales and spin-offs speak volumes.

Progoff, Ira. *At a Journal Workshop: Writing to Access the Power of the Unconscious and Evoke Creative Ability*. New York: Tarcher/Putnam, 1975. Offers guidance on the art of dialoguing.

Reik, Theodor. *Listening with the "Third" Ear*. Farrar, Straus, and Giroux, 1983. Listening for the metacommunications in another's speech.

Rinpoche, Sogyal. *The Tibetan Book of Living and Dying*. San Francisco: HarperSanFrancisco, 1992. A look at Tibetan beliefs and practices associated with death.

Selye, Hans. *Stress Without Distress*. New York: Signet, 1974. Describes the "Relaxation Response," a popularized version of an Eastern meditation practice.

Sheldrake, Rupert. *The Presence of the Past: Morphic Resonance and the Habits of Nature*. New York: Vintage Books, 1988. Introduces the idea of morphic fields and how they account for animal and human behavior.

Teeguarden, Iona Marsaa. *The Joy of Feeling: Bodymind Acupressure—Jin Shin Do*. Tokyo: Japan Publications, 1987. A good introduction to the theory and application of Traditional Chinese Medicine (TCM) and its integration with Western psychological theory.

Walsch, Neale Donald. *Conversations with God*. New York: G. P. Putnam's Sons, 1996. A reputedly "channeled" conversation with an aspect of God.

Weil, Andrew, M.D. *8 Weeks to Optimum Health: A proven program for taking full advantage of your body's natural healing power*. New York: Alfred A. Knopf, 1997.

Wilber, Ken. *A Theory of Everything*. Boston: Shambhala, 2000. A brief synopsis of the evolution of consciousness, past, present, and future. Also includes Wilber's theory of differing ways of knowing.

Wolf, Fred Alan, Ph.D. *The Body Quantum: The New Physics of Body, Mind, and Health*. New York: Macmillan Publishing Company, 1986. "The processes governing the living movement of matter in the body arise through . . . the observing of one's own body, consciously and unconsciously." (from dust jacket)

Yogananda, Paramahansa. *The Autobiography of a Yogi*. Los Angeles: Self-Realization Fellowship, 1959. An incredibly beautiful account of the life and death of an Indian yogi.

Zipes, Jack, trans. *The Complete Fairy Tales of the Brothers Grimm*. New York: Bantam Books, 1987.

RECOMMENDED WEB SITES:

www.dr.weil.com—Dr. Andrew Weil's Web site.

www.holisticmedicine.com—A guide to practitioners and products.

www.indoc.org—The official site for the South Bay doctors in California who are practicing independently of HMOs and managed care organizations.

www.mdheal.org—Official site for the Foundation for Integrated Medicine.

www.nih.com—National Center for Complementary and Alternative Medicine. This site is currently under construction.

http://ohioline.osu.edu/hyg-fact/5000/5279.html—A Web site with information about the psychological and behavioral effects of birth order.

www.ralphmoss.com and www.cancerdecisions.com—Both sites are run by Ralph Moss, an independent researcher who has the latest information on healing options for every type of cancer, though some information is only available by subscription.

www.tldp.com—The Web site for *The Townsend Letter for Doctors and Patients*, a review of the latest research on alternative medicine.

Index

Page numbers in *italics* indicate illustrations.

Books of Related Interest

The Power of Emotion
Using Your Emotional Energy to Transform Your Life
by Michael Sky

The Healing Power of the Mind
Practical Techniques for Health and Empowerment
by Rolf Alexander, M.D.

Emotional Healing through Mindfulness Meditation
Stories and Meditations for Women Seeking Wholeness
by Barbara Miller Fishman, Ph.D.

Hildegard of Bingen's Spiritual Remedies
by Dr. Wighard Strehlow

Aromatherapy for Healing the Spirit
Restoring Emotional and Mental Balance with Essential Oils
by Gabriel Mojay

Gesundheit!
Bringing Good Health to You, the Medical System, and Society through
Physician Service, Complementary Therapies, Humor, and Joy
by Patch Adams, M.D., with Maureen Mylander

When Healing Becomes a Crime
The Amazing Story of the Hoxsey Cancer Clinics and the Return
of Alternative Therapies
by Kenny Ausubel

Vibrational Medicine
The #1 Handbook of Subtle-Energy Therapies
by Richard Gerber, M.D.

Inner Traditions • Bear & Company
P.O. Box 388
Rochester, VT 05767
1-800-246-8648
www.InnerTraditions.com

Or contact your local bookseller